BEST OF THE BEST

More **Fast&Fabulous**

FIVE ★ STAR

⑤INGREDIENT *(or less!)*

RECIPES

D0472917

BEST OF THE BEST
More Fast & Fabulous
FIVE ★ STAR
5 INGREDIENT
RECIPES (or less!)

Gwen McKee
and
Barbara Moseley

QUAIL RIDGE PRESS
Preserving America's Food Heritage

Library of Congress Cataloging-in-Publication Data

McKee, Gwen.
  Best of the best more fast & fabulous five-star 5-ingredient (or less!) recipes /
    Gwen McKee and Barbara Moseley. — 1st ed.
    p. cm.
    Includes index.
    ISBN-13: 978-1-934193-43-3
    ISBN-10: 1-934193-43-7
  1. Quick and easy cooking. 2. Cooking, American. I. Moseley, Barbara. II. Title.
TX833.5.M443 2010
641.5973—dc22   2010033653

On the cover: Grilled Chicken Pepper Toss, page 179; Marinated Tomato Salad, page 80;
Buttermilk Yeast Rolls, page 41

Design by Cyndi Clark
Cover photos by Greg Campbell

Printed in Canada

First edition, April 2011

Disclaimer: The sizes of commercial food packages and cans often change, generally becoming
smaller. In many cases, using a slight variation of the size specified in the recipe will affect the
outcome so slightly as to be barely or not noticeable at all. The cook will have to make this
determination. If there is a significant variation in the quantity specified in the recipe, it may
necessitate reducing the amount of that ingredient found in the next larger size package or can.

QUAIL RIDGE PRESS
P. O. Box 123 • Brandon, MS 39043
info@quailridge.com • www.quailridge.com

Contents

Gwen McKee and Barbara Moseley love to play golf.
"Cooking out of this cookbook allows more time for fun."

Preface

How many times have you wanted to prepare a dish or a meal without a lot of ingredients or a lot of complicated preparations? If you answered, "All the time," or, "Quite often," or even, "Sometimes," then this cookbook is for you!

When I saw the movie *Julie and Julia*, I was inspired to make some of the recipes. Having met Julia Child in Nashville years ago at a book symposium where I was cooking gumbo, I became a devoted fan. (Imagine the thrill of *me* autographing my *Little Gumbo Book* for Julia Child!) Not long ago, I got out my old original cookbook of hers and endeavored to cook her "Beef Bourguignonne." It took many steps, and I spent the whole day preparing it. It was indeed delicious, but my lifestyle does not often lend itself to that much time and effort in the kitchen, and I put the book back on the shelf.

Barbara Moseley and I created *More Fast & Fabulous Five-Star 5-Ingredient (or Less!) Recipes* to be your friend in the kitchen—you will want to reach for it every day. With nearly 600 recipes to choose from—that's a whole lot of recipes—this cookbook offers you a great variety of easy-to-prepare dishes, most of which contain ingredients you already have in your pantry or refrigerator. The book offers fresh ideas for sprucing up old favorites, as well as learning about new recipes. You are sure to find dozens among the 580 recipes that you will tag to use over and over again. Barbara and I are pleased to present to you a huge selection of recipes that go one step further than fast: *They all taste great!*

Since 1978, we have been bringing you the delicious results of our search for recipes that are people pleasing, family friendly, and easily doable. In this companion volume of our wildly successful *500 Fast & Fabulous Five-Star 5-Ingredient Recipes*, we decided to make it even easier by using not more than five, often four, or three, and sometimes just two ingredients. And, yes, there are even a couple of one-ingredient recipes (pages 33 and 34) that transform a single ingredient into something yummy.

Though many of these recipes might be described as ideas rather than recipes because they are so short and simple, aren't most recipes just ideas anyway? To learn from? To compare with? To build on? To improve with what you have on hand? Of course they are. It has long been my opinion that recipes serve as guides. You can usually sub different soups, gelatins, pastas, seasonings, etc., because you don't have exactly what's called for, or because you prefer pecans over walnuts, or you want to appease a diet by using low-fat instead of regular, and on and on. These recipes give you the basics of method and consistency and temperatures so that you can feel free to wander a little off the written path, though they can all stand alone quite well.

While all these recipes have five ingredients or less and are easy to prepare, some take a little longer to get on the table because of a crockpot cooking it all day, or a Bundt cake taking an hour to bake, or a brisket cooking several hours to perfection. But prep time is minimal, and your shopping time is shorter by way of fewer ingredients.

All of these recipes have five or less ingredients, the only exceptions being salt and pepper to taste, which we figure everybody keeps on hand. Sometimes a recipe calls for a package mix "made per package directions," which we realize involves one or two more ingredients. But these were recipes we knew you would want included, figured you would have the ingredient(s) called for, or knew you could buy a ready-made cake or the like by choice.

In addition, we have included Editor's Extras below many of the recipes to suggest different methods, ingredients, enhancements, garnishes, and hints. As in our first *5-Ingredient* cookbook, our recipes have come from friends, relatives, cookbook lovers, and customers who have graciously shared their favorite recipes with us, as well as sharing our own creations and experiments and antics in the kitchen, which, I might add, is ongoing.

And for all of you who love to read cookbooks, you are in for an extra treat. Our sidebar theme was *five* in the first book, and this time, it is *fast*. Some of the fastest will get even faster . . . records are made to be broken. It was interesting and amusing for us to gather. We hope you enjoy our "lagniappe."

We thank the many people who have sent us recipes, and our wonderful staff, but we also want to thank you, our fans, who love our cookbooks and go to our website, *www.quailridge.com*, and our Facebook page to help us make our cookbooks better with your comments and feedback . . . we love you right back.

Need a little help in the kitchen? With *More Fast & Fabulous Five-Star 5-Ingredient (or Less!) Recipes*, we are right in there with you. Enjoy!

Gwen McKee

More Fast
and
Fabulous

FIVE ★ STAR

Beverages & Appetizers

The world is changing very **fast**. Big will not beat small anymore. It will be the **fast** beating the slow.

—*Rupert Murdoch*

Cran-Raspberry Iced Tea

Cool and refreshing.

4 small tea bags
4 cups boiling water
1 (12-ounce) can frozen cranberry-raspberry
    juice concentrate, thawed
4 cups cold water

Put tea bags in boiling water; cover and steep 5 minutes. Remove tea bags and refrigerate tea.

Just before serving, mix cranberry-raspberry concentrate with cold water in a big pitcher; stir in tea. Serve over ice. Makes 2½ quarts.

Golden Party Punch

A party in a punch bowl.

1 (6-ounce) can frozen lemonade
1 quart prepared orange juice
1 (12-ounce) can apricot nectar
1 (46-ounce) can pineapple juice
2 (12-ounce) cans Sprite, chilled

Combine all ingredients except Sprite. Chill. Just before serving, add Sprite. Makes 24–30 cups.

Pink Punch with Punch

Pretty and delicious!

1 (6-ounce) can frozen limeade concentrate, thawed
4 cups cranberry juice
4 cups lemon-lime beverage, chilled
1–2 cups orange vodka
⅓ cup Grand Marnier

Combine limeade and cranberry juice in large punch bowl. Add lemon-lime drink slowly down side of bowl. Add vodka and Grand Marnier; stir gently to mix. Serve over ice cubes and garnish with lime slices. Makes 14 servings.

Big Easy Hurricane Punch

A taste of New Orleans.

1 (48-ounce) can Hawaiian Punch
1 (12-ounce) can frozen orange juice concentrate
1 (6-ounce) can frozen lemonade
⅔ cup sugar
Good dark rum to taste

Mix punch, juices, and sugar in large pitcher or bowl. Fill hurricane or tall glasses with crushed ice and add 1–2 jiggers rum per glass; fill with punch. Garnish with stemmed cherries and half orange slices. Serves 6–8.

Kentucky Slush

1 (6-ounce) can frozen lemon juice concentrate
1 (6-ounce) can frozen orange juice concentrate
3 (6-ounce) cans water
6 ounces bourbon

Blend together and freeze in big plastic container. Ready to pour from the freezer. Serves 6.

Baqdad

Not bad, Dad . . . in fact, delicious!

1 ounce rum
1 ounce Galliano liqueur
5 ounces fresh orange juice

Pour rum and Galliano over ice cubes in a champagne glass. Add orange juice and stir. Garnish with orange or lime slices. Serves 1.

Margarita Martini

5 ounces gold tequila
1 ounce Cointreau
1 ounce Grand Marnier (or Blue Curaçao)
2 ounces freshly squeezed lime juice
Simple syrup* to taste

Fill a shaker with ice. Add all and shake! Serves 1–2.

*Boil a cup of water with 2 tablespoons sugar stirred in.

Perky Pineapple Daiquiris

Icy and refreshing.

1 (11-ounce) can crushed pineapple with juice
1 (6-ounce) can frozen limeade or lemonade
1 limeade can rum
1 tablespoon sugar
Ice cubes

Blend all but ice in blender 20 seconds. Fill blender with ice cubes and blend on high till crushed; add a little water if too thick. Serves 4–6.

Liquid Breakfast

Easy breakfast to get you going.

2 tablespoons smooth peanut butter
1¼ cups milk
½ ripe banana
1 scoop protein powder (optional)

Combine all ingredients in blender and blend for a few seconds. Serves 1.

Purple MooMoo

Refreshing fruity drink; great for breakfast.

2 big scoops vanilla yogurt or ice cream
1 cup purple grape juice
2 cups milk

Whirl all ingredients in blender. Serves 4–6.

Editor's Extra: Add ice cubes or crushed ice for a smoothie moo moo.

Fastest Pitcher in Baseball?

Fans, researchers, historians, and even the players argue all the time about who was the **fastest** pitcher of all time. The most widely quoted response is Nolan Ryan, whose **fastball** was "officially" clocked by the *Guinness Book of World Records* at 100.9 mph in a game played on August 20, 1974, versus the Detroit Tigers—a record that's still included in the book.

Instant coffee was invented in 1901 by Satori Kato, a Japanese scientist working in Chicago. Kato introduced the powdered substance in Buffalo, New York, at the Pan-American Exposition. George Constant Louis Washington developed his own instant coffee process shortly thereafter, and first marketed it commercially (about 1910). The Nescafé brand, which introduced a more advanced coffee refining process, was launched in 1938.

Perfect Irish Coffee

Makes your eyes smile.

1¼ ounces Irish whiskey
2–3 sugar cubes
¾ cup strong coffee
Sweetened whipping cream, lightly whipped

Pour whiskey over sugar cubes into a warmed glass; add hot coffee. Float cream on top by pouring it over the back of a teaspoon. Serves 1.

A Rich Cuppa Mocha

This is sooo good.

4 cups strong coffee
½ cup sweetened condensed milk
½ cup chocolate syrup

In saucepan over low heat, whisk coffee, milk, and syrup. When hot, pour into mugs and garnish with whipped cream and chocolate shavings (optional). Store leftovers in frig. Serves 6.

Happy Holidays Cider

Warming and wonderful.

⅔ cup red cinnamon candies
1 gallon apple cider or juice
2 teaspoons whole cloves
2 cinnamon sticks
1 medium orange, halved, sliced

Add candy to cider in large pot and cook over medium heat till candy is dissolved. Pour into heat-proof punch bowl or crockpot. Add cloves and cinnamon sticks, but remove before serving. Float orange slices on top. Serves 12–16.

Blender Piña Colada Fruit Dip

Surround this with fresh fruit bites.

1 (8-ounce) can crushed pineapple, undrained
½ cup vanilla yogurt
1 (3-ounce) package coconut instant pudding
¾ cup milk
1 tablespoon rum, or ½ teaspoon rum flavoring

Blend all in blender for 30 seconds. Refrigerate, covered, at least an hour to chill. Serve with fresh fruit for dipping. Offer toothpicks. Makes 2 cups.

In-A-Hurry Fruit Dip

1 (8-ounce) tub soft cream cheese (plain,
pineapple, or strawberry)
1 (7-ounce) jar marshmallow crème

Mix together well. Serve with bite-size fresh fruit of choice. Makes 2 cups.

Amaretto Fruit Dip

Make this a day ahead and refrigerate.

1 (8-ounce) package cream cheese, softened
2 cups powdered sugar
2 tablespoons sour cream
2 tablespoons amaretto

Mix all together well. Serve with fruits of choice. Makes 1⅔ cups.

Tropic Fruit Bowl

Perked-up fresh-cut fruit.

¼ cup light rum
¼ cup orange juice
1 teaspoon almond or coconut extract
3 cups melon balls, pineapple chunks, grapes,
or other fresh fruit

Combine rum, orange juice, and extract; pour over fruit in a pretty glass bowl and refrigerate 30 minutes. Serve with wooden picks.

Melinda's Jarlsberg Cheese Dip

This really needs to be doubled, because it disappears fast!
—Melinda Burnham

2 cups shredded Jarlsberg cheese
¾ cup mayonnaise
½ cup very finely chopped purple onion

Mix all ingredients well and serve with tortilla chips or Melba toast. Serve warm or cold.

Howdy Padnah Dip

1 pound ground pork sausage
1 (10¾-ounce) can Cheddar cheese soup
1 (8-ounce) jar taco sauce
1 (1-pound) box processed American cheese,
cubed

Brown and drain sausage well. Add remaining ingredients, and heat till cheese is melted, stirring often. Serve hot with firm chips or French bread cubes.

Quick Queso

1 (10¾-ounce) can cream of mushroom soup
¾ cup shredded Monterey Jack cheese
1 (4-ounce) can chopped green chiles
1 teaspoon garlic powder

Heat soup and cheese till cheese melts. Add chiles and garlic powder, and serve warm with Fritos, tostadas, or blue corn chips.

Tex-Mex Bacon Cheese Dip

½ pound bacon, cooked, crumbled
1½ pounds Mexican Velveeta cheese, cubed
1 bunch green onions, chopped

Combine ingredients in microwave dish. Heat 1–2 minutes on HIGH; stir till cheese is melted. Serve with tostadas or Fritos Scoops.

Crockpot Taco Dip

Great for parties; this goes a long way.

1 pound lean ground beef
1 pound Velveeta, cubed
1 package taco mix
1 (15-ounce) can chili with beans

Brown ground beef; drain. Put all in a small crockpot and simmer slowly, stirring occasionally till cheese melts. Serve with tostadas or Fritos Scoops.

Fastest Land Animal

The cheetah is able to achieve speeds upwards of 70 mph. It cannot, however, maintain this speed for very long, and prey that has a bit of luck can "wear down" the cheetah if it can avoid it for 10–15 seconds.

Fastest Bird

Talk about a dive bomber! The peregrine falcon (historically known as the "Duck Hawk" in North America) is the **fastest** bird on record, reaching horizontal cruising speeds of 40–55 mph and not exceeding speeds of 65–68 mph. When stooping, the peregrine flies at much greater speeds, however, varying from 99–273 mph!

Easy Mexican Dip

1 (8-ounce) carton guacamole dip
2 tomatoes, diced
3 green onions with tops, diced
3 tablespoons chopped black olives
½ cup shredded mozzarella cheese

Spread guacamole on dinner plate. Layer remaining ingredients; chill. Serve with tortilla chips.

Blue Cheese Lovers' Spread

½ cup blue cheese, room temperature
½ cup cream cheese, softened
3 tablespoons finely chopped celery
Freshly ground black pepper to taste

Combine all; chill. Serve with crackers of choice.

Editor's Extra: Good to mold on a small plate; pour ¼ cup ranch dressing or buffalo wing sauce over top.

Romano Bread Dip

A great beginning to any meal . . . and all through it. So good with any crusty Italian bread.

⅔ cup olive oil
⅓ cup canola oil
1½ teaspoons minced garlic
1 teaspoon red pepper flakes
⅔ cup grated Romano cheese

Mix first 4 ingredients. Put a tablespoon or 2 of Romano cheese onto a salad plate and pour 2–3 tablespoons oil mixture on top. Dip bread pieces into mixture to get some of each. Replenish as needed.

30-Second Roasted Red Pepper Dip

1 (7-ounce) jar roasted red peppers, drained
1 tablespoon snipped fresh basil (or 1 teaspoon dry)
1 (16-ounce) container sour cream
1 garlic clove

Whisk all in blender 30 seconds until thoroughly blended. Add some black pepper, if desired. Serve right away with bagel chips or crackers, or store in frig in airtight container.

Sun-Dried Tomato Dip

¼ pound mozzarella cheese
½ cup sun-dried tomato pesto
¼ cup grated Parmesan cheese

Cut cheese into ½-inch cubes and place in oven-safe serving dish. Bake at 400° for 4–6 minutes until cheese begins to melt. Spoon pesto over cheese; top with Parmesan cheese and return to oven for another 1–2 minutes. Serve with Fritos Scoops or party crackers. Serves 6–8.

French Onion Corn Dip

2 (15-ounce) cans southwestern-style corn
1 (2-cup) package shredded Cheddar cheese
½ cup French onion dip
½ cup mayonnaise

Combine all ingredients and chill. Great served with tortilla chips or large scoops.

Editor's Extra: If you have any left over, mix a few tablespoons with a can of drained tuna—great sandwich or cracker spread.

Yummiest Corn Dip Ever

2 (11-ounce) cans Mexicorn, drained
1 cup mayonnaise
1 cup shredded sharp Cheddar cheese
1 cup grated Parmesan cheese
1 (10-ounce) can mild Ro-Tel, drained

Mix all together in greased casserole dish and bake at 350° about 25 minutes (or microwave on HIGH 7–10 minutes). Serve hot with tostadas or Fritos Scoops.

Pepperoni Shroom Dip

⅔ cup chopped pepperoni
1 (4-ounce) can sliced mushrooms, drained
2 cups shredded Swiss or mozzarella cheese
⅔ cup Miracle Whip
½ cup sliced black olives

Stir all together and place in Pam-sprayed baking dish. Bake in 400° oven 15 minutes. Serve with bagel chips or small party crackers.

Not Your Ho-Hum Hummus

This is so good with warm pita points. —*Courtney Jernigan*

1 (15-ounce) can chickpeas, drained, reserve liquid
1 tablespoon olive oil
1 tablespoon minced garlic
2 teaspoons cumin
¾ teaspoon lemon pepper

Combine all ingredients, except liquid, in a food processor and blend until well combined. Check for consistency; if too thick, add a tablespoon at a time of reserved liquid.

Editor's Extra: For an extra kick, add red pepper flakes or Cajun seasoning.

Hot-Happy Cheese Balls

These have a spark, but make them to your own degree of hotness . . . just be sure to warn your guests if you get hot-pepper happy.

1 (6.5-ounce) tub garlic and herbs spreadable cheese
1 stick butter, softened
1 cup all-purpose flour
1½ teaspoons Worcestershire
⅛ teaspoon cayenne pepper, or more

Mix all together well and roll into olive-sized balls. Bake on baking sheet at 450° for 8–10 minutes. These freeze well before baking, so are a good make-ahead, heat-when-you're-ready, pop-in-your-mouth appetizer. Makes a bunch!

Fastest-Running Flying Bird

The North American roadrunner has been clocked at 26 mph when pursued by an automobile. A coyote can run 43 mph. But in the cartoon, Wile E. Coyote could never catch his nemesis, Road Runner, who always outsmarted him.

Animal Speeds

- Peregrine falcon
  200+ mph

- Cheetah
  70 mph

- Quarter horse
  55 mph

- Lion
  50 mph

- Greyhound dog
  45 mph

- Coyote
  43 mph

- Ostrich
  40 mph

- Rabbit (domestic)
  35 mph

- Cat (domestic)
  30 mph

- Grizzly bear
  30 mph

- White-tailed deer
  30 mph

- Human
  27.89 mph

- Elephant
  25 mph

- Squirrel
  12 mph

- House mouse
  8 mph

- Great tortoise
  0.17 mph

- Garden snail
  0.03 mph

Nutty Cheese Log

1 (8-ounce) bar Cheddar cheese, grated
1 (8-ounce) package cream cheese, softened
1 teaspoon chili powder
1 teaspoon minced garlic
¾ cup finely chopped pecans

Mix all well with your hands. Shape into a log and roll up in wax paper; refrigerate. Serve on cheese board with crackers, or slice thinly and fan next to cracker fan.

Bodacious Cheese Spread

1 pound sharp Cheddar cheese, grated
16 slices bacon, fried crisp, crumbled
12 green onions, including tops, chopped
1 cup slivered almonds, toasted
2 cups mayonnaise

Mix all ingredients in order given. Good to spread on most crackers or Melba rounds. Makes a lot.

Baked Brie in Pastry

1 sheet frozen puff pastry, thawed
1 (4½-ounce) round Brie cheese, chilled

Preheat oven to 375°. Roll pastry to approximate 11x14-inch rectangle. Cut out 2 (6-inch) rounds. Place Brie on one round; top with remaining round. Paint edges with a little water and pinch together to seal well. Bake on pie pan about 15 minutes till pastry is lightly browned and puffed. Serve with crackers and/or green apple slices.

Editor's Extra: Offer heated caramel apple dip or hot pepper jelly.

Pizzazzy Salmon Spread

1 (8-ounce) package cream cheese, softened
¼ cup heavy cream
1 green onion, thinly sliced
1 teaspoon horseradish
4 ounces smoked salmon, gently shredded

Mix all together. Add salt and pepper or lemon pepper to taste, if desired. Serve with crackers of choice for an hors d'oeuvre, or on thin bagels or rye bread or toast for a lunch treat.

Editor's Extra: A drop or two of liquid smoke can make unsmoked salmon taste smoked. Also, a few drops of Tabasco gives it a little more pizzazz.

Blue Cheese Asparagus Finger Rolls

Impressive and different.

1 (8-ounce) bar cream cheese, softened
4 ounces blue cheese
10–12 slices thin-sliced bread
1 (15-ounce) can asparagus spears
3 tablespoons butter, melted

Blend cheeses well (may have to add a tad of milk to make easily spreadable). Cut crusts from bread; roll out thin. Spread with cheese mixture. Roll an asparagus spear into each bread slice. Brush with butter; slice into three pieces diagonally. (Freezable at this point.) Bake at 350° only a few minutes until golden brown. Makes 30–36.

Classic Artichoke Spread

Can't beat an old classic.

1 (14-ounce) can artichoke hearts, drained, finely chopped
1 cup mayonnaise
1 (8-ounce) package shredded mozzarella cheese
¾ cup grated Parmesan cheese
1 teaspoon garlic powder

Combine all and spread in lightly greased pie dish. Bake at 350° for 25–30 minutes. Serve with pita chips or crackers or tostadas.

Perky Sausage Balls

The sauce is so tasty and a favorite at parties.

2 pounds sausage, hot or mild
1 cup sour cream
1 (9-ounce) bottle chutney, chopped
⅓ cup dry sherry

Shape sausage into small balls; place on baking pan and bake 15 minutes or more at 350° till browned; drain. Heat remaining ingredients and put into chafing dish; add sausage balls. Spear with toothpicks. Makes about 40.

Comfort Food Sausage Balls

These are best when prepared and frozen the night before.
This is one of my favorite comfort foods. —Courtney Jernigan

1 cup Bisquick
1–1½ cups grated sharp Cheddar cheese
1 (16-ounce) roll sage pork sausage

Mix all ingredients. (You will have to really use your hands to get all of the Bisquick mixed in, but it's worth it!) Roll into 1-inch balls and place in a large freezer bag on a cookie sheet. Place cookie sheet with sausage balls in freezer so balls will freeze flat and not get mashed.

When ready, preheat oven to 350° and cook desired amount of sausage balls on a nonstick or greased baking sheet for 25–35 minutes or until browned on top.

If in a hurry with no time to freeze overnight, simply cut cook time in half, 12–17 minutes at 350°. Yields about 2 dozen.

Sausage Biscuit Squares

These are always popular.

1 pound lean pork sausage, hot or mild
2 cups grated sharp Cheddar cheese
3 cups biscuit mix

Mix all thoroughly with hands. Pat into square pan and bake at 350° for 15–20 minutes till brown. Cut into squares.

Speed of Light

The speed of light (usually denoted "c") is a physical constant. Its exact value is 299,792,458 meters per second, often approximated as 300,000 kilometers per second or 186,000 miles per second. It is a constant, whether it comes from a moving source such as a speeding car's headlights, or an unmoving source such as a ceiling light.

Oh-So-Simple Cranberry Meatballs

Good served over rice or pasta, too.

2 (8-ounce) bags frozen original flavor meat-balls
1 (15-ounce) can crushed pineapple, undrained
1 (16-ounce) can jellied cranberry sauce

Cook meatballs in a skillet over medium heat with just a little oil, turning them till they brown.

Mix pineapple and cranberry sauce in a bowl, then pour over meatballs, stirring gently to coat all sides. Heat till bubbly, then cover and lower heat till ready to serve. May keep warm and serve from crockpot, if desired. Makes about 48.

Bacon Bows

Try it! You'll like it!

Bacon strips
Club crackers

Cut bacon into thirds. Wrap each third around one club cracker. Place seam side down onto microwave-safe dish that has been lined with paper towels. Prepare as many as desired. Microwave till bacon is done. Be careful—crackers will be very hot. Drain on paper towels.

Jalapeño Devils

A kicky heavy hors d'oeuvre.

1 dozen fresh whole jalapeños
½ pound block Monterey Jack cheese
2 pounds ground pork sausage
1 cup seasoned bread crumbs

Using rubber gloves, wash jalapeños, leaving stems intact. Slit peppers lengthwise with paring knife. Gently remove all seeds. Next, cut cheese into ¼-inch strips and stuff into peppers. Set aside.

Make a dozen sausage patties, and shape each one around to entirely cover a pepper. Roll peppers in bread crumbs and place on baking pan. Bake 25–30 minutes at 350°, till sausage is done. Makes 12.

Bacon-Wrapped Stuffed Jalapeños

Preparation is a little tedious, but worth it! Make as many as you dare.

Jalapeño peppers
Cream cheese, softened
Grated Cheddar cheese
Bacon slices, halved

With rubber gloves on, slice jalapeños in half lengthwise and remove all seeds. Combine cheeses; fill peppers with cheese mixture. Wrap bacon around each pepper and fasten with toothpick. Bake at 350° till bacon is done.

Oh Soy Good Glazed Drummettes

1 (6-ounce) bottle lite soy sauce
1 teaspoon dry mustard
1 tablespoon brown sugar
½ teaspoon garlic salt
2 dozen chicken drummettes

Mix all ingredients except drummettes. Pour over drummettes in lightly greased 9x13-inch baking pan; refrigerate overnight, covered.

Preheat oven to 325°. Bake, uncovered, 1½ hours, basting several times.

Sunset Drummettes

¼ cup ketchup
¼ cup apricot preserves
½ cup steak sauce of choice
12 chicken drummettes

Whisk ketchup, preserves, and steak sauce until smooth; brush chicken with this sauce. Grill chicken over medium heat about 20 minutes, turning and brushing with remaining sauce. Makes 12 appetizers.

Fiery Onion Chicken Tenders

½ cup hot wing sauce
2 cups crushed French-fried onions
1½ pounds boneless skinless chicken breasts,
cut into strips

Place sauce and French-fried onions in separate dishes. Dip chicken strips in sauce, then in crushed onions, coating well. Place on baking sheets sprayed with cooking spray, then spray tops. Bake 10–12 minutes in 400° oven till tender. Serve hot. Serves 8–12.

Barney's Deli Appetizer

My husband Barney loves good tasty food, but is not one to do any cooking. Or shopping. Recently he has been going to the supermarket with me and comes home with "surprises." He serves ME a cracker with assorted goodies on it, and we declared this to be a favorite. —Gwen McKee

Shaved ham or turkey
Cheese of choice, sliced to fit crackers
Boar's Head Spicy Mustard
Crackers of choice
Bread and butter pickles (optional)

Put generous amounts of ham or turkey, cheese, and mustard on each cracker. A pickle slice is optional.

Hot Sausage Mushroom Caps

½ (8-ounce) package cream cheese, softened
30 small mushrooms, cleaned, stems removed
½ (1-pound) roll hot pork sausage

Place ½ teaspoon cream cheese into each mushroom cap. Press a small ball of sausage on cream cheese. Broil 5 inches from heat source till sausage is done.

Fastest Rising Mountain

In Pakistan, the Nanga Parbet is growing taller, at a rate of 9.27 inches per year. Part of the Himalayan Plateau, this mountain formed when India began colliding with the Eurasian continental plate between 30 and 50 million years ago.

Top 5 Fastest Cars in the World

1. SSC Ultimate Aero: 257 mph, 0–60 in 2.7 seconds

2. Bugatti Veyron: 253 mph, 0–60 in 2.5 seconds

3. Saleen S7 Twin-Turbo: 248 mph, 0–60 in 3.2 seconds

4. Koenigsegg CCX: 245 mph, 0–60 in 3.2 seconds

5. McLaren F1: 240 mph, 0–60 in 3.2 seconds

Cheesy Chile Won Tons

2 cups grated Monterey Jack cheese
1 (4-ounce) can chopped green chiles
1 package won ton skins
Oil for frying

Mix cheese and green chiles. Put a teaspoonful on each won ton skin and fold like an envelope. Fry a few at a time in 2 inches of hot oil, turning once, till golden brown. Drain. Makes 20.

Bacon-Cheese Finger Sandwiches

1 (10¾-ounce) can Cheddar or nacho cheese soup, undiluted
20 slices sandwich bread
20 slices bacon, cut in half

Spread soup on 10 slices of bread. Top with the remaining slices. Cut each into 4 "fingers" and wrap with a half slice of bacon. Put on broiler pan and bake 45–60 minutes at 250°. Makes 40.

Pimento Shrimp Salad/Spread

2 (7-ounce) cans shrimp, drained, chopped
1 (8-ounce) package cream cheese, softened
¼ cup finely chopped green onions
¼ cup chopped pimento
Mayonnaise

Mix ingredients well, using enough mayonnaise to form a smooth mixture. Serve on lettuce, on bread, or with crackers.

Luscious Stuffed Shrimp

A great combination of zesty flavors.

½ (8-ounce) package cream cheese, softened
4 teaspoons creamy horseradish
1 tablespoon grated Parmesan cheese
1 pound large shrimp, cooked, peeled, deveined

Combine cream cheese, horseradish, and Parmesan cheese till well blended. Butterfly shrimp along outside curve. Pipe or stuff about 1 teaspoon cream mixture into each shrimp. Place on serving platter and serve with cocktail sauce, if desired. Keep refrigerated till serving time. Makes about 24.

Fried Zucchini Sticks

The secret is in the batter.

1 pound medium-size zucchini
⅔ cup flour
1 cup water
1 teaspoon Creole seasoning
Grated Parmesan (optional)

Cut zucchini into French-fry-like sticks. Mix flour with water till smooth; add seasoning. Pat sticks dry. In a frying pan with ¾ inch oil, or deep fryer, heat oil. Dip zucchini in batter and fry in hot oil until golden brown on both sides. Remove with slotted spoon onto paper towels and sprinkle with Parmesan cheese, if desired. Serve immediately. Serves 4.

Tiny Party Pizzas

1 pound pork sausage
⅔ cup chopped onion
1 pound processed American cheese, cubed
¼ cup tomatoes and green chiles (Ro-Tel)
Party rye bread

Brown sausage with onion; drain. Melt cheese in heavy pot; add tomatoes, and meat. Put a teaspoonful on a party rye bread slice on a cookie sheet; heat in 350° oven till bubbly, about 15 minutes. Serves 16.

Pepperoni Crescents

1 (8-ounce) package crescent rolls
40 or so small rounds pepperoni, cut up
2 pieces string cheese, quartered
¾ teaspoon Italian seasoning, divided
¼ teaspoon garlic salt

Separate crescent rolls into triangles. Place pepperoni bits on triangles, then a piece of cheese at long side of each triangle. Sprinkle with half the Italian seasoning; roll up starting with long side; pinch seams together to seal. Place on cookie sheet and sprinkle with remaining Italian seasoning and garlic salt. Bake at 375° for 10–12 minutes, or till golden brown. Makes 8, or 24 when cut into thirds.

Pepperoni Roll-Ups

1 (13½-ounce) package refrigerated pizza crust
½ (8-ounce) package cream cheese, softened
1 cup shredded mozzarella/provolone mixture
⅓ cup finely chopped pepperoni

Roll out pizza crust. Mix remaining ingredients together and spread on crust. Roll pizza crust back into a log and bake in 350° oven until golden brown, 15–20 minutes. Let roll rest before slicing.

Flavorful Homemade Potato Chips

1 cup all-purpose flour
1–2 packets dry salad dressing mix (garlic,
   Italian, ranch)
3 large red-skin potatoes

Mix flour and dressing mix of your choice in sealable plastic bag. Slice potatoes into thin round disks; pat dry. Add in batches to seasoned flour; shake well. Arrange on baking sheet; continue with remaining slices. Refrigerate potatoes about 20 minutes.

In heavy-bottomed skillet, add enough oil to go about halfway up the sides; heat to 375°. Fry potato slices in small batches until crisp. Remove and drain on paper towels. Season to taste with salt and pepper. Serves 6 or more.

Sweet Potato Chips

2 sweet potatoes, peeled, cut into ⅛-inch slices

Soak potato slices in cold water to cover for 30 minutes. Preheat oven to 400°. Spray baking sheets with nonstick cooking spray. Drain potatoes and pat dry. Lay in single layer on cookie sheet and bake for 20–25 minutes, or until chips are crisp. May sprinkle with kosher salt or powdered sugar, if desired. Serves 6 or more.

#1 Fast Food Chain

The McDonalds Corporation is located in Oak Brook, Illinois.

• One out of every eight workers in the United States has, at some point, worked at a McDonald's restaurant.

• It is the nation's largest purchaser of beef, pork, and potatoes, and second largest of chicken (KFC is #1).

• It has replaced Coca Cola as the world's most famous brand, but serves Coca Cola in its establishments.

• It operates more playgrounds—designed to attract children and their parents to its restaurants—than any other private entity in the world.

Lemon Pepper Pita Chips

Pita bread
Margarine
Lemon pepper seasoning

Cut pita bread open and spread margarine well on both sides. Sprinkle generously with lemon pepper. Cut into strips; bake on baking pan at 325° for 15 minutes. Serve as a snack or with soup.

Cinnamon-Butter Coated Walnuts

1 stick butter
4 cups walnut halves
1 cup sugar
1 tablespoon cinnamon
¼ cup water

Combine butter and walnuts in skillet; stir. In another skillet, heat remaining ingredients. After a few minutes, combine mixtures, stirring till walnuts are coated. Spread in single layer on foil. When cool, store in glass jars. Makes 4 cups.

Parmesan Delights

A one-ingredient recipe that is easy-please-y delicious.

2 cups freshly grated Parmesan cheese

Put tablespoons of grated cheese as neatly as possible on parchment paper or a silicone baking mat on a cookie sheet with several inches of space between them. Lower the pile, then gather the excess cheese closer to each mound. Bake in a 300° oven 5–6 minutes, till starting to bronze.

If desired, mold immediately over a small glass bottom to shape into cups. They will harden quickly into cups that are so nice for holding dips. Adding a sprinkle of black pepper, paprika, or cayenne before baking is interesting as well.

Zippy Pecans

3 tablespoons butter
3 cloves garlic, minced
1–2 teaspoons Tabasco
3 cups pecan halves

Melt butter in skillet; add garlic, Tabasco, and salt to taste; cook over medium heat 1 minute. Toss pecans with butter mixture and spread nuts in a single layer on a baking pan. Bake for 1 hour at 250°, stirring occasionally, until crisp.

Perfect Toasted Pecans

As simple as it seems, you need good instructions so you won't burn these precious babies.

1–2 tablespoons butter
2 cups pecan halves

OVEN METHOD:
Preheat oven to 400°. Melt butter in a glass bowl in the microwave 20–25 seconds on #5 power, then pour pecans in and stir well to coat. Spread nuts onto a baking pan and bake 5 minutes, stirring after 3. Another minute or 2 achieves darker toasting, but chancy, so watch so it doesn't burn. Ovens are different, so watch those precious pecans.

PAN METHOD:
Melt the butter in a large skillet on medium heat. Add pecans and stir every minute or so for about 4 minutes till toasted.

MICROWAVE METHOD:
Sprinkle a little salt on pecan halves; spread in a big Pyrex dish (no butter). Microwave on HIGH 2 minutes; stir. Zap another minute; stir. Continue doing this in 1-minute increments till they taste roasted, up to 9 minutes total, if necessary.

Editor's Extra: Other nuts toast the same, chopped nuts, too.

Nutty Stuffed Celery

6 stalks celery
1 tablespoon butter, softened
1 tablespoon blue cheese, softened
½ (8-ounce) package cream cheese, softened
2 tablespoons finely chopped, toasted nuts

Use a vegetable peeler to remove outside strings from celery stalks. Cut into 2-inch pieces. Combine butter and cheeses and mash together. Spread mixture in celery sticks; sprinkle nuts on top. Makes about 24.

Editor's Extra: Try pistachios, sunflower seeds, walnuts, or pecans.

Easy Pepper Jelly

1 green bell pepper
1 jalapeño pepper
1½ cups cider vinegar
6½ cups sugar
1 (6-ounce) bottle liquid fruit pectin

Pulse stemmed and cleaned peppers in food processor well (and green food coloring, if desired). Pour into saucepan, add vinegar and sugar, and boil 5 minutes. Remove from heat; stir in fruit pectin till it starts to jell. Pour into sterile jars and seal. Good served over block of cream cheese with crackers.

More Fast and Fabulous

FIVE ★ STAR

Bread & Breakfast

Deluxe Cornbread

1 cup self-rising cornmeal mix
2 eggs, beaten
1 (8-ounce) can cream-style corn
1 cup sour cream
⅓ cup oil or bacon grease, divided

Mix all ingredients except 1 tablespoon oil. Pour 1 tablespoon oil into 9-inch pan or iron skillet; heat slightly, then pour batter into pan. Bake at 400° about 20 minutes. Serves 6.

Dash-Of-Spice Cornbread

An incredible lift to an old favorite.

3 tablespoons oil, divided
1½ cups yellow self-rising cornmeal mix
1½ cups buttermilk
1 large egg
1 teaspoon Mrs. Dash Extra Spicy Seasoning

Heat oven to 400°. In cast-iron skillet add 1 table-spoon oil; heat in oven. Combine cornmeal mix, buttermilk, egg, seasoning, and remaining 2 table-spoons oil. Pour mixture into hot oil in skillet and bake 20–25 minutes, or till brown. Serve hot with butter. Serves 8.

Editor's Extra: Turn the oven to broil the last minute or two for a lovely browned, crustier top. But watch it carefully, or set a timer for one minute to check.

Cheesy Broccoli Cornbread

A meal in itself!

1 (6-ounce) box cornbread mix
1 cup finely chopped onion
2 cups grated Cheddar cheese
4 eggs
1 (10-ounce) box frozen chopped broccoli,
thawed, well drained

Mix all ingredients together with a little salt and pepper, and place in greased 9x13-inch pan. Bake 25 minutes at 350° till golden brown. Serves 6–8.

Drop-Dead-Delicious Butter Biscuits

Absolutely delicious!

1½ sticks butter, softened
2 cups self-rising flour
1 (8-ounce) carton sour cream

Mix butter and flour till crumbly. Add sour cream and mix well. Drop by spoonfuls into ungreased tiny muffin tin. Bake at 450° for 8–10 minutes. Makes 40–50 bite-size biscuits.

Mayonnaise Biscuits

2 cups self-rising flour
3–4 tablespoons mayonnaise
½–1 cup milk

Mix all ingredients in mixing bowl about 2 minutes. Pour into Pam-sprayed 12-cup muffin pan. Bake in 425° oven 10 minutes or till golden brown.

Fastest Aircraft

The North American X-15 is the **fastest** manned aircraft, setting the world speed record at 4,520 mph. Not only is the X-15 the **fastest** piloted aircraft ever, it is the highest flying. The X-15 was launched from under the wing of a B-52. Thrust was obtained from one engine that produced 70,400 lbs at maximum altitude.

The R-71 Blackbird is the **fastest** jet aircraft in the world, setting the world speed record at 2,293 mph.

Avatar is the **fastest** movie to gross $500 million, taking only 32 days. (It took *Titanic* 45 days.) James Cameron's *Avatar* is the biggest movie in box-office history. It was the first movie ever to gross over $2 billion, grossing $2.05 billion worldwide as of February 2010.

Easy Scratch Biscuits

1¼ cups self-rising flour, divided
⅔ cup buttermilk
3 tablespoons canola oil, divided

Mix 1 cup flour and buttermilk with fork; add 2 tablespoons oil. Sprinkle with additional flour while kneading, till not sticky. Roll out and cut with biscuit cutter, or pat out biscuits in your hands. Pour 1 tablespoon oil on baking sheet. Turn biscuits over in oil and place on pan. Bake at 425° for 12–20 minutes, depending on thickness, till golden brown. Makes 6–10.

Rise 'n Shine Biscuits

2¼ cups self-rising flour
1 tablespoon sugar
½ cup butter-flavored shortening
⅔ cup milk
1 egg, beaten

In mixer, combine flour and sugar. Add shortening, mixing till mixture resembles coarse meal. Combine milk and egg; add to flour mixture, and stir till moistened. On floured board, pat or roll to ½-inch thickness. Cut with biscuit cutter; brush top with a little melted butter, if desired. Bake at 325° for 10–12 minutes.

Whipping Cream Biscuits

1¾ cups self-rising flour
1 cup whipping cream

Heat oven to 450°. Mix flour and whipping cream with fork until dough leaves side of bowl and rounds up into a ball. (If dough is too dry, mix in 1–2 teaspoons additional whipping cream.) Turn dough onto lightly floured, cloth-covered board. Knead lightly 10 times, sprinkling with flour if dough is too sticky.

Roll or pat dough ½ inch thick. Cut with floured 2-inch biscuit cutter. Place about 1 inch apart on ungreased cookie sheet. Bake until golden brown, 10–12 minutes. Immediately remove from cookie sheet. Serve hot. Makes 12 biscuits.

Editor's Extra: May make into pan biscuits by patting dough evenly in ungreased, 8x8-inch-square pan. Bake 12–15 minutes. Cut into 2-inch square biscuits. Makes 16.

Buttermilk Yeast Rolls

1 package dry yeast
3 cups self-rising flour
1–2 tablespoons sugar
½ cup shortening
1 cup buttermilk

Dissolve yeast in 2 tablespoons warm water; set aside. Blend flour, sugar, and shortening with pastry cutter. Mix yeast and buttermilk; add gradually to flour mixture; store in greased bowl several hours or overnight. Pinch off and shape into rolls; let rise 30–40 minutes. Bake 15 minutes at 425°.

Crescent Roll Bundt Bread

A new twist on crescent rolls. Easy, easy, easy, and so delicious.

⅓ cup butter
3 (8-count) tubes crescent rolls

Melt butter in Bundt pan while oven is preheating to 350°. Open tubes, but do not disturb rolls at all. Place the 3 roll tubes end to end in the melted butter; bake about 30–35 minutes. Turn out on a plate and slice with serrated knife.

Editor's Extra: Heat some strawberry jam to drizzle over—or try melted chocolate chips!

Four French Loaves

2½ cups all-purpose flour
1 tablespoon (or 1 package) baker's yeast
1 teaspoon honey
1 cup warm water

Combine flour, yeast, and a little salt in mixing bowl. In separate bowl, combine honey and water thoroughly; stir in flour mixture. Cover and place in a warm place to rise approximately 10 minutes. Preheat oven to 350°.

Punch dough down and shape into 4 small loaves. Place on a lightly oiled cookie sheet and bake 20–30 minutes till crust is light golden brown. Serve warm. Yields 4 small loaves.

Ice Cream Bread? Yes!

Incredible, but true.

1½ cups self-rising flour
2 cups butter pecan ice cream, softened

Combine flour and ice cream; mix well. Pour into 2 (3x5-inch) loaf pans, greased and floured. Bake 20–25 minutes in 350° oven. Cool before slicing.

Editor's Extra: May use any flavor ice cream, but not low-fat. Drizzle with fruity or chocolate ice cream sauce.

The world is moving so **fast** these days that the man who says it can't be done is generally interrupted by someone doing it.
—*Elbert Hubbard*

Sliced Onion Bread

Great with barbecue.

1 long loaf French or sourdough bread
½ cup butter, softened
1 Vidalia or other sweet onion, thinly sliced

Cut bread into ¾-inch slices partially through bottom, leave about ¼-inch bottom. Butter each slice and place a slice of onion in between. Press loaf together and wrap in foil. Bake at 450° for 15 minutes.

Crunchy Nacho Twists

Good with or without a dip!

⅔ cup crushed Doritos
1 (11-ounce) can refrigerated breadsticks

Pour Dorito crumbs on a shallow cookie sheet. Separate dough into strips, roll in Doritos, pressing to stick to all sides. Twist each strip twice and place on a baking pan, pressing ends down firmly. Bake 13–15 minutes at 375° till golden brown. Serve warm.

Cheesy Butter Roll-Ups

1 loaf thin-sliced white bread, crusts removed
1 (8-ounce) jar Cheez-Whiz
2 sticks butter, melted
1 (8-ounce) package grated Parmesan cheese

Flatten each piece of bread with a rolling pin. Spread slices thinly with Cheez-Whiz, not too heavily. Roll up each bread piece like a crescent roll. Quickly dip into melted butter. Roll in grated Parmesan cheese. Bake on cookie sheet at 350° for 10–12 minutes till lightly browned. Freeze immediately on tray. May cut in half when partially frozen and store in freezer bags.

When ready to serve, reheat in 375° oven 12–15 minutes.

Stuffed Honey Buns

Sticky, gooey good!

2 (8-ounce) cans refrigerated crescent rolls
1 (8-ounce) package cream cheese, cut into 16 cubes
¼ cup butter, melted
3 tablespoons honey
½ teaspoon almond extract (optional)

Spray muffin cups. Unroll crescent rolls; divide into triangles. Place 1 cube at base of each triangle and roll up to enclose cheese. Bring ends of crescents together, forming balls. Combine remaining ingredients and spoon into bottom of cups. Place balls of dough in each cup. Bake at 350° for 15–20 minutes. Makes 16.

Breadstick Pretzels

1 (11-ounce) roll refrigerated breadsticks
3 tablespoons egg substitute (or 1 beaten egg)
Coarse sea salt
1 cup French onion cheese spread

Cut each breadstick in half lengthwise. Twist carefully like tying a loose knot to look like a pretzel. Place on ungreased cookie sheet; brush with beaten egg; sprinkle with salt. Bake at 375° about 14 minutes until bronze. Serve with French onion, or any other kind of cheese spread for dipping. If dip is too stiff, dilute with a little milk.

Cranberry-Orange-Zucchini Bread

Bring greater taste and texture to a muffin mix.

1 (17-ounce) package cranberry-orange muffin
   mix
1½ cups shredded zucchini
1 cup water
1 teaspoon ground cinnamon
1 teaspoon freshly grated orange peel
   (optional)

Preheat oven to 350°. Combine muffin mix and remaining ingredients in medium bowl; stir just till moistened. Spoon batter into Pam-sprayed 8-inch loaf pan. Bake 40 minutes or till toothpick comes out clean. Cool 5 minutes before removing from pan; remove from pan and cool completely. Nice to offer soft butter or cream cheese with slices. Serves 12–16.

Miracle Whip Banana Bread

Very simple to whip up!

1 cup Miracle Whip
1 cup mashed ripe bananas
2 cups all-purpose flour
¾ cup sugar
2 teaspoons baking soda

Heat oven to 350°. Combine Miracle Whip and bananas. In separate bowl combine flour, sugar, and soda. Add dry ingredients to banana mixture; mix well. Pour into greased loaf pan. Bake 55–65 minutes. Let stand 10 minutes. Remove from pan and cool completely.

Easy Club Soda Waffles

Light, delicious . . . and no need to beat egg whites.

1⅓ cups club soda
1 egg
2 cups Bisquick mix
½ cup oil

Mix all ingredients well. Bake in waffle iron till golden. Serve hot with topping of your choice. Makes about 6.

Corn Waffles

1 (6-ounce) package corn muffin mix
½ cup creamed corn
1 teaspoon maple flavoring
1–2 tablespoons milk

Prepare muffin mix according to package directions; stir corn and flavoring into batter. Add 1–2 additional tablespoons milk to make batter correct consistency for waffles. Preheat waffle iron. Pour in batter, close lid quickly, and do not open until steaming stops. Repeat with remaining batter. Makes 4.

Editor's Extra: Great to serve topped with creamed chicken, salsa, or sour cream. Syrup is good, too, but especially blueberries.

Eggnog French Toast

A holiday breakfast treat.

½–⅔ cup eggnog
4 thick slices French bread
2 tablespoons oil
Powdered sugar

Pour eggnog into a shallow bowl. Dip both sides of bread into eggnog, then cook in oil about 2½ minutes or until golden. Turn bread. Cook about 1½ minutes more, or until golden.

Transfer to a serving plate. Sprinkle with powdered sugar. Makes 2 servings.

Fastest Flightless Bird

The ostrich can run 45 mph.

Fastest Train

The **fastest** passenger train is France's TGV (tres grande vitesse, which means "very great speed"). On a test run in 1990, it barreled along the tracks at a top speed of 456 mph while carrying just a few cars. The record for a train on a scheduled route goes to a TGV that travels on a line from Paris to Strasbourg in France. In 2007, it reached a top speed of 357 mph.

Blender Apple Pancakes

1⅓ cups milk
2 eggs
2 cups biscuit mix
¼ teaspoon cinnamon
1 apple, peeled, chopped

Blend all in blender till smooth. Pour batter onto hot greased griddle. Turn when bubbly. Serve with syrup or whipped topping. Makes 10–12 pancakes.

Raspberry Coffee Cake

1 (3-ounce) package cream cheese, softened
¼ cup butter, softened
2 cups Bisquick
⅓ cup milk
Seedless raspberry preserves

Cut cream cheese and butter into Bisquick. Add milk; mix well. Place on floured board and knead about 9 times. Roll out to 8x13-inch rectangle. Spread raspberry preserves down short center. On each side of pastry, cut several 2-inch fingers 1 inch apart. Fold across preserves in criss-cross method. Bake at 425° for 12–15 minutes. May top with powdered sugar glaze, if desired. Serves 4–6.

Cow Punchin' Chili 'n Eggs

Great way to stretch leftover chili into a breakfast delight.

1 medium onion, chopped
1 teaspoon chopped garlic
2 tablespoons butter
1 cup chili without beans (canned or leftover homemade)
4–5 eggs, beaten

Sauté onion and garlic in butter till soft. Stir in chili till hot. Add eggs; stir over medium heat till set. Season with salt and pepper to taste. Roll in tortillas, if desired, and serve with picante sauce. Or they're good on their own. Serves 4–6.

Green Chile Cheese Soufflé

These spruced-up eggs are great for company.

2 cups shredded sharp Cheddar cheese, divided
1 (7-ounce) can chopped green chiles
5 eggs
⅛ teaspoon baking soda
2 dashes cayenne pepper

Put 1 cup cheese in buttered casserole, then all of chiles, then remaining cheese on top of chiles. Beat eggs with baking soda, cayenne, and a little salt to taste; pour over cheese. Bake in 400° oven 35 minutes or till set. Bring on the picante sauce! Serves 4–6.

Poblano Frittata

A breakfast boost.

4 eggs
¼ cup milk
12 ounces bulk pork sausage
1 small poblano pepper, seeded, chopped (use gloves)
1 cup shredded Cheddar cheese

Whisk eggs and milk together; set aside. Heat skillet over medium-high heat. Add sausage and stir till browned. Remove with slotted spoon to paper towels. Cook pepper in same skillet 2 minutes; return sausage. Add egg mixture and stir to blend. Cover and cook over medium heat till eggs are almost set, about 10 minutes. Sprinkle cheese over top; broil 4 inches from heat 2 minutes till cheese melts. Serve immediately. Serves 4.

Bagelicious Breakfast Treats

You'll love this quick and easy all-in-one breakfast treat.

2 hard-boiled eggs
2 strips bacon, crisply fried, crumbled
1 tablespoon mayonnaise
1 bagel, split, toasted

Peel and dice eggs (mash with fork, if desired). Combine crumbled bacon with eggs; add mayonnaise and salt and pepper to taste. Place half the mixture on each toasted bagel half. May spread bagel half with butter, if desired. Serves 2.

A Bacon 'n Egg Burrito

Better plan on making a bunch of these.

1 egg, scrambled
2 strips bacon, fried
1–2 tablespoons shredded Monterey Jack cheese
1 flour tortilla, warmed
Salsa to taste

Roll egg, bacon, and cheese in warm tortilla. Serve with salsa. Serves 1.

Editor's Extra: Cooked, crumbled, or sliced chorizo may be substituted for bacon for a spicier burrito. Fried, grated or cubed potatoes can be added.

Eggs Florentine

A brunch treat.

2 tablespoons butter, softened
1 cup shredded Swiss cheese
8 eggs
1 (6-ounce) bag baby spinach, stems removed
½ cup whipping cream

Preheat oven to 350°. Spread butter in 8-inch baking dish. Sprinkle half the cheese over butter. Break eggs carefully onto cheese. Pierce yolks with a fork, but don't stir eggs; leave them separate. Salt and pepper to taste. Place spinach on eggs and pour cream over all. Sprinkle with remaining cheese. Bake at 350° for 25–30 minutes, until eggs are set and casserole is bubbly. Serves 4–6.

Fastest Nonconventional Vehicle

In 2003, an unmanned sled train propelled by a rocket motor traveled 6,453 mph—more than eight times the speed of sound—at Holloman Air Force Base in New Mexico.

Fastest Motorcycle

American Dave Campos rode Easyrider, his 23-foot-long streamliner-style motorcycle, at an average speed of 322.87 mph. He sped his supercycle over the Bonneville Salt Flats in Utah in 1990.

Fastest Production Motorcycle

The Suzuki GSX1300R Hayabusa is reported to reach a speed of up to 194 mph.

Three-Man Beer Omelettes

What? Yes. Just do it.

6 eggs
⅓ cup beer
½ teaspoon Tabasco
3 tablespoons butter, divided
3 tablespoons grated Parmesan cheese, divided

Blend eggs with beer and Tabasco. In medium pan over medium heat, melt 1 tablespoon butter. When melted, pour ⅓ of egg mixture in. Tilt pan and lift the edge of the omelette with a spatula so the unset portion can run to the bottom. When set, sprinkle with 1 tablespoon cheese. Fold over and slide onto plate to serve. Repeat with remaining egg mixture. Serves 3.

Potato Breakfast Bake

½ (12-ounce) package frozen seasoning blend (onions, peppers, celery)
4 tablespoons oil, divided
8 eggs
3 cups mashed potatoes or frozen shredded hashbrowns
½ cup grated Parmesan cheese

Preheat oven to 325°. In a large oven-safe skillet at medium-low heat, sauté the seasoning blend in 2 tablespoons oil till vegetables are tender, stirring often. Remove from skillet.

In a large bowl, whisk together eggs, potatoes, and cheese. Stir in sautéed vegetables. In the same skillet, heat remaining oil, and raise temperature to medium. Cook egg mixture in skillet only until bottom is set. Carefully transfer skillet to preheated oven. Bake about 20 minutes until fully set. To serve, cut in wedges. Serves 6–8.

"Souper" Soufflé

½ pound shredded Cheddar cheese
1 (10¾-ounce) can cream of mushroom soup
4 eggs, separated
½ teaspoon Greek or Cajun seasoning
4–6 slices bacon, cooked, crumbled

Melt cheese with soup in a medium saucepan over medium-low heat. Add beaten egg yolks and salt and pepper to taste to soup mixture. Add seasoning. Beat egg whites till stiff; slowly fold into soup mixture. Pour into a greased 9x13-inch casserole dish. Sprinkle with crumbled bacon. Bake in a slow oven (315°) for 30–45 minutes. Serves 6–8.

A Honey of a Soufflé

4 eggs, separated
1 teaspoon flour
¾ (8-ounce) package cream cheese, softened
1 cup sour cream
¼ cup honey

In mixer bowl, beat egg yolks till creamy; add flour. Beat in cream cheese and sour cream till smooth; add honey gradually. In another bowl, beat egg whites till stiff but not dry, and fold into first mixture. Pour into ungreased 1½-quart soufflé dish. Place baking dish in pan halfway full of water; bake in preheated 300° oven 1 hour. Serves 4–6.

Chile Rellenos

Keeping the batter on the chile a problem? Not anymore.

6 canned whole green chiles
½ pound Jack or Cheddar cheese
3 eggs, separated
¼ cup vegetable oil

Cut a slit down the side of each chile and remove the seeds. Leave the stem on. Place a long slice of cheese, the size of the chile, down the inside.

Beat egg whites until stiff. Lightly beat the yolks and fold into whites. Season with salt and pepper.

In a large frying pan, heat oil. With a large spoon, place a long dollop of egg batter, the size of the chile, in the hot oil. Now gently place the chile on the bed of batter, and drizzle some more batter on top. Flip over to cook golden brown on both sides. Serve at once with sour cream and salsa, if desired. Serves 2–4.

Sausage Brunch Bread

1 loaf frozen bread dough, thawed
1 pound hot pork sausage, cooked, crumbled
1 cup grated Parmesan cheese
2 eggs, lightly beaten

Grease a 9-inch bread pan. Spread dough on floured parchment paper. Mix sausage, Parmesan, and eggs. Spread mixture down center of bread dough. Fold sides of dough in toward center; seal. Fold ends in and seal. Brush top of dough with sausage drippings or butter. Place dough in prepared bread pan; cover with towel and let rise to top of pan. Bake at 350° for 30 minutes, or until golden brown. Let sit 5 minutes before slicing. Serves 6.

Quick Hash and Biscuits

1 (1-pound) package beef tips
1 large onion, chopped
1 (10¾-ounce) can cream of mushroom soup
1 (10-count) tube refrigerated biscuits

Cook beef tips and onion in enough water to cover. When tender, shred or cut meat into small pieces. Add mushroom soup and place in 9x13-inch baking dish. Place biscuits on top of meat mixture and bake in 350° oven 20 minutes, till biscuits are brown.

Leftover Rice with Eggs

Not only does it stretch your eggs, it tastes great!

½–1 cup leftover cooked rice
3 eggs, beaten
½ cup sharp Cheddar cheese
2 strips crispy fried bacon, crumbled

Combine rice, eggs, and cheese; pour into lightly greased skillet. Scramble as you would scrambled eggs. Add salt and pepper to taste. Sprinkle crumbled bacon on top. Serves 3.

Creamy Cheesy Grits

3¾ cups boiling water
1 teaspoon salt
1 cup grits
1 cup grated Cheddar cheese
½ cup milk

Bring water and salt to a boil. Stir in grits and cook slowly 10–15 minutes, covered, stirring occasionally. Add cheese and milk, blending thoroughly. Heat till cheese melts. Leave covered till served. Serves 6.

Does cold water boil faster than hot water?

No. Water boils at 212°F or 100°C at sea level. The closer you start to the boiling point, the shorter time it takes to reach it. This assumes, of course, you are using the same amount of heat in both cases.

Great Links of Flavor

2 dozen small breakfast sausage links
1 onion, halved, sliced
2 apples, cored, unpeeled, sliced thinly
¾ cup brown sugar

Brown sausages in baking pan in 325° oven 15 minutes; drain grease. Arrange onion and apple slices in layers on top of sausages; sprinkle brown sugar on top; return to oven for 40 minutes. Serves 6–8.

Sugar-Glazed Bacon Strips

These are scary good. May be made a few hours ahead.

1 pound bacon, strips cut in half
1 (1-pound) box brown sugar

Pat each half slice of bacon on both sides with brown sugar, covering well. Place on rack with pan under. Bake at 325° for 15–25 minutes till browned and fat is cooked out. Place bacon on wax paper to cool. Serve at room temperature.

Mose's Sausage Gravy

1 pound bulk pork sausage, hot or mild
¼ cup all-purpose flour
2 cups milk

Cook sausage and crumble while cooking. Drain grease when brown; leaving ¼ cup drippings in pan. Add flour to drippings; cook 2–3 minutes. Stir in milk and salt and pepper to taste. Add crumbled sausage; cook till thick. Serve over hot biscuits.

Hot Mushroom Roll-Ups

1 cup chopped mushrooms
2 tablespoons butter
1 tablespoon all-purpose flour
¼ cup half-and-half
8 slices fresh bread, crusted

Sauté mushrooms in butter 3 minutes. Add flour and half-and-half; cook till thick; cool. Cut bread slices in half. Spread with mixture; roll, then secure with toothpick. Toast 2–3 minutes under broiler. Serve while hot. Makes 16.

Editor's Extra: Add a tad of chopped parsley if you want a little color.

Fajita Wraps

2 onions, sliced
2 green bell peppers, sliced
1 (10-ounce) package cooked fajita steak strips
12 (7-inch) flour tortillas, warmed
Prepared guacamole (optional)

Sauté onions and peppers till slightly wilted and tender. Add fajita strips and toss to heat. Place filling on tortillas and season to taste; add guacamole, if desired. Roll up and serve, or wrap in foil, if not serving immediately.

Cheese and Glazed Onion on Rye

This is a WOW sandwich! A grill pan makes it look as good as it tastes.

½ red onion, thinly sliced
1 teaspoon olive oil
4 slices dark rye bread
6 ounces boursin or havarti cheese, sliced
½ cup prepared coleslaw

Cook onion slices until tender in oil in skillet, about 5 minutes on medium heat. Pile onto 2 pieces of bread with cheese and coleslaw. Top with other bread slices. Place sandwiches in skillet, pressing down with spatula (or use sandwich press). Cook on medium heat 4 minutes on each side, till bread is toasty brown. Serves 2.

Editor's Extra: Any kind of cheese will make this sandwich differently delicious.

Provolone Tuna Melts

1 (12-ounce) can tuna, drained
¼ cup diced roasted red peppers
2 tablespoons bottled ranch dressing
4 slices Italian bread, lightly toasted
8 slices provolone cheese

Combine tuna, peppers, and dressing. Spread evenly over toasted bread; top with cheese. Place on baking sheet, and broil till cheese melts. Serves 4.

Fast &

Perky Turkey Paninis

½ cup Dijonnaise
1 (3-ounce) package cream cheese, softened
8 (½-inch) slices sour dough bread
1 pound thinly sliced turkey
8 slices Colby-Jack cheese

Combine Dijonnaise and cream cheese. Spread on one side of all bread slices. Top 4 slices with turkey and cheese. Cover with remaining bread slices, spread side down. Coat electric skillet or grill with cooking spray. Grill sandwiches 5 minutes, pressing down with spatula or press, till cheese melts. Makes 4 sandwiches.

Editor's Extra: You can sub a spoon of Dijon mustard added to mayo for the Dijonnaise.

Apple Cheddar Ham Panini

2 tablespoons honey mustard
8 slices whole-wheat bread
2 apples, thinly sliced
8 slices sharp Cheddar cheese
16 slices thin deli ham

Preheat press or grill. Spread honey mustard on each slice of bread. Layer apple slices, cheese, and ham over 4 slices of bread. Top each with remaining bread slices. Coat press with vegetable spray. Grill each sandwich 3–5 minutes or till bread is golden brown and cheese has melted. Cut in half to serve. Makes 4 servings.

Fastest Eater

The star-nosed mole handles its food for an average of 230 milliseconds before eating it. (Doesn't sound like a picky eater.)

Fresh Basil-Tomato Pizza

Great for lunch or supper.

1 ready-made pizza crust
2 cups grated mozzarella cheese
3–4 Roma tomatoes, thinly sliced
1 bunch fresh basil, finely chopped
Olive oil or mayonnaise

Preheat oven to 375°. Spread crust with mozzarella cheese. Place sliced tomatoes on top of cheese. Scatter basil over tomatoes; drizzle with olive oil or dab with mayo. Sprinkle with black pepper, if desired. Bake 15–20 minutes, till cheese is melted and crust is browned. Serves 6–8.

Bacon 'n Tomato Rounds

6 pieces white bread, cut in large rounds
3 bacon slices, cooked crisp, crumbled
1–2 tablespoons mayonnaise or soft cream cheese
2 ripe tomatoes, sliced in thirds
Salt to taste

Toast bread rounds slowly till lightly browned and slightly dried out. Combine bacon and mayonnaise; spread over rounds. Place a tomato slice on each; salt to taste and add a sprinkle of chopped parsley, if desired. Serve open faced. YUM!

Good Morning Fruit Rolls

1 (12-ounce) tube refrigerated cinnamon roll dough
1 cup apple pie filling
½ cup dried cranberries

Reserve icing packet from cinnamon rolls. Place rolls in ungreased muffin cups. Bake 8 minutes at 400°. Remove from oven and press an indention in center of each. Combine apple pie filling and cranberries, and fill indention. Bake an additional 5 minutes till golden brown; remove to wire rack; cool a few minutes before drizzling with icing. Serve while warm.

Simple Watermelon Rind Preserves

2 quarts thick watermelon rind, cut in ½-inch cubes
½ teaspoon salt
6 cups sugar
3 cups water
2 tablespoons lemon juice

Boil rind in salted water to cover till clear and soft. Drain well. Boil sugar, 3 cups water, and lemon juice. Boil till thick, then add rind and boil till transparent and syrup thickens. Fill jars and seal.

Sweet Tomato Jelly

5 pounds ripe tomatoes
8 cups sugar
2 lemons, thinly sliced

Scald tomatoes so peelings can be easily removed. Peel and chop tomatoes, and place in large bowl. Cover with sugar and let stand overnight.

Next day, drain juice into a large stockpot. Bring to a boil, and boil until threads form. Add tomatoes and lemons. Allow to cool. When thick and clear, pack in hot sterilized jars and seal.

Two-Ingredient Strawberry Jam

It can't get much easier than this!

4 cups fresh strawberries, hulled, sliced
4 cups sugar

Bring strawberries to a boil over medium heat with sugar (no water). Boil for 4 minutes. Pour into casserole dish, and let sit overnight. Pour into hot sterilized jars, and seal.

More Fast and Fabulous

FIVE ★ STAR

Soups, Chilies, & Stews

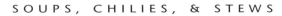

Easy Cheesy Broccoli Soup

1 (10-ounce) package frozen chopped broccoli
2 tablespoons butter
1 (10¾-ounce) can Cheddar cheese soup
2 cups milk or cream

Cook broccoli as directed; drain. In blender, combine broccoli, butter, and soup. Heat with milk in saucepan, being careful not to boil. Serves 4–6.

Alfredo Soup

1 (15-ounce) jar Alfredo sauce
1½ cups chopped broccoli
1½ cups chicken broth or milk
1 teaspoon minced garlic

Heat all together in saucepan till broccoli is cooked—do not boil. Serve with crackers or grainy toast. Serves 4–6.

Editor's Extra: Add a cup or so of cooked noodles, if desired.

Shortcut Roasted Red Pepper Soup

2 (12-ounce) jars roasted red peppers
1 (14-ounce) package frozen mirepoix (onions, celery, carrots)
2 cloves garlic, minced
2 (14½-ounce) cans chicken broth

Combine all ingredients in stockpot with salt and pepper to taste, and simmer for 25–30 minutes. Purée soup, ½ at a time, in blender or food processor. Serve with croutons or French bread. Serves 6–8.

Editor's Extra: If you want a thicker soup, add ¼ cup instant mashed potatoes to mixture.

Mom's Tater Soup

This is just plain good!

6 potatoes, peeled, chopped
4 slices bacon, chopped
1 cup diced onion
Milk

Boil potatoes in water, just to cover, till tender. Do not drain. Fry bacon till crisp. Remove from skillet; set aside. Add onion to skillet and sauté till clear. Add to potatoes and water; add salt and pepper to taste. Gradually add milk till desired consistency is reached. Simmer till creamy and heated through. Serves 6.

Pepper Jack Potato Soup

Open your "pizazzy" taste buds.

3 (10¾-ounce) cans potato soup
2 (12-ounce) cans evaporated milk
1½ cups shredded Pepper Jack cheese, divided
6 slices bacon, fried crisp, crumbled

Combine potato soup and milk in large saucepan. Cook over medium heat 6–8 minutes. Stir in ½ of cheese till melted. Season with salt and pepper, if desired. Pour into soup bowls and sprinkle with remaining cheese and crumbled bacon. Serves 6.

Creamy Hashbrown Soup

1 (32-ounce) bag southern-style hashbrowns, or O'Brien potatoes
1 (10¾-ounce) can cream of onion soup
1 (10¾-ounce) can cream of celery soup
1 cup plain dry coffee creamer
1 pound Velveeta cheese or Mexican Velveeta, cubed

Place frozen hashbrowns in large soup pot; cover with water. Bring to a boil, reduce heat and simmer 15 minutes. Mix soups and creamer in a bowl. Add to hashbrowns, stir well, and simmer 5 minutes more. Add cheese; stir till cheese melts. Serves 8–10.

Editor's Extra: You can add cut-up cooked chicken to this or leftover cooked vegetables.

Fresh Potato-Veggie Soup

5 medium potatoes, peeled, diced
3 medium onions, diced
1 (16-ounce) package frozen mixed vegetables
2 (10¾-ounce) cans cream of celery soup
1 pound Velveeta cheese, cubed

Cook potatoes and onions in water to cover till tender. Add frozen vegetables; cook about 5 minutes. Add soup and cheese and cook another 5 minutes, stirring to melt cheese. Serves 6–8.

A good potato peeler peels potatoes and carrots **faster** than a knife. And a food chopper with a cutter gives you more uniform pieces . . . it's a bit **faster**, too.

See-More Carrot Soup

6 carrots, scraped, coarsely chopped
1 potato, peeled, coarsely chopped
1 (12-ounce) package frozen seasoning blend
1 (14½-ounce) can chicken broth
½ cup milk

Combine carrots, potato, seasoning blend, and broth in saucepan; bring to a boil. Cover and simmer till vegetables are tender. Place mixture in blender and purée till smooth; add milk and blend. Season to taste. Heat and serve. Serves 6.

Fab more taste

Creamy Artichoke Soup

2 (10¾-ounce) cans cream of mushroom soup
1 pint whipping cream (or half-and-half)
1½ cups chicken broth
½–1 teaspoon Tabasco
2 (14-ounce) cans artichoke hearts, drained

In large bowl, combine soup, cream, broth, and Tabasco. In food processor or blender, place ½ the artichokes and ½ the soup mixture and process till puréed. Pour into stockpot. Repeat with remaining ingredients. Pour all in stockpot and heat over low heat till heated through. Serves 6–8.

Toucan Asparagus Soup

Definitely not for the birds, this two-can soup is quick to fix and is quite elegant.

2 (14-ounce) cans Cheddar cheese soup
2 (14-ounce) cans cream of asparagus soup
2 (14-ounce) cans asparagus spears, undrained
1 soup can white zinfandel
2 asparagus cans light cream

Purée all in blender except cream. Heat to boiling, stirring frequently. Stir in cream; lower heat. Serve when heated through. Serves 10–12.

Zappo French Onion Soup

1 cup thinly sliced onions
¼ stick butter
1 (14½-ounce) can beef broth
2 slices French bread, toasted
½ cup shredded Swiss cheese

Combine onions and butter in glass bowl; cook 2½ minutes on HIGH in microwave; stir. Add broth and cook on HIGH 2½ minutes more; stir. Put in 2 microwave-safe soup bowls; place bread slices on top; sprinkle with cheese. Cook, uncovered, 40 seconds on HIGH till cheese melts. Serves 2.

Three-zy Spinach Soup

1 (10-ounce) box frozen, chopped spinach,
** thawed**
1 (10¾-ounce) can cream of chicken soup
1–1½ cups milk

Squeeze out all liquid from spinach. In a medium saucepan, heat soup and milk to desired consistency on medium heat; add spinach and stir to blend. Season to taste; cook till heated through. Serves 4–6.

Bean and Tomato Soup

Great served with hot cornbread.

1 (10¾-ounce) can bean and bacon soup
1 cup milk
1 (14½-ounce) can diced tomatoes with onions,
** celery and green peppers, undrained**

Combine soup and milk in saucepan till smooth; heat, but do not boil. Add tomatoes and stir well. Heat thoroughly; do not boil. Serves 3–4.

Great Northern Bean Soup

**1 (12-ounce) package frozen seasoning blend
   (peppers, onions, celery)**
¼ cup butter
1 (14½-ounce) can diced tomatoes, undrained
**2 (16-ounce) cans Great Northern beans,
   drained**
2½ cups cubed ham

Sauté seasoning blend in butter till tender. Add tomatoes and one can beans. Mash remaining can of beans before adding along with ham. Add water if needed for consistency. Salt and pepper to taste. Cook over medium-low heat about 30 minutes, stirring often. Serves 6.

Smoked Ham and Bean Soup

3 (15-ounce) cans white beans, drained, divided
1½ cups chicken broth, divided
½ cup chopped fully cooked smoked ham
⅓ cup chopped celery
⅓ cup chopped onion

Purée 1 can beans with ½ the chicken broth in blender. Bring to a boil in stockpot with remaining ingredients; cover and simmer 15 minutes. Season with salt and pepper, if desired. Serves 4–6.

Fast &

Speedy Tamale Soup

2 (16-ounce) cans pinto beans
1 (15-ounce) can whole-kernel corn
1 (14½-ounce) can diced tomatoes
1 (14-ounce) can chicken broth
1 (15-ounce) can tamales, sliced

Mix first 4 ingredients in saucepan. Gently stir in tamales. Simmer over medium-low heat 15–20 minutes, till heated through. Serves 8–10.

The trouble with talking too **fast** is you may say something you haven't thought *through* yet.

—Gwen McKee

Crockpot Corn and Sausage Chowder

1 pound smoked sausage, sliced
3 cups frozen hashbrowns
1 (15-ounce) can creamed corn
2 cups water
1 (10¾-ounce) can cream of chicken soup

Pan-fry sausage, then place in crockpot with slotted spoon. Top with hashbrowns. Combine corn, water, and soup; mix well; pour over hashbrowns. Cover and cook on LOW 8 hours. Serves 6–8.

Italian Chili Soup

1 (11¼-ounce) can chili beef soup
1 (10-ounce) can beef consommé
1 soup can water
1 (10-ounce) package frozen Italian-style
   vegetables in sauce

Combine all ingredients and cook over medium heat till heated through. Serves 6.

The term **"quick as a wink"** was first recorded in 1825. One wink = 1/10 second.

Quick-As-A-Wink Chili

1 pound ground chuck
1 (14½-ounce) can diced tomatoes
1 (10-ounce) can Ro-Tel tomatoes
1 (16-ounce) can baked beans with onions, liquid included
1 (1¼-ounce) package dry chili mix

Brown ground beef; drain and add remaining ingredients; simmer 15–30 minutes. Serve over macaroni, if desired. Grated cheese is good on top. Serves 6–8.

Editor's Extra: Good subbing red beans, too.

Cheesy Baked Chili

1 (15-ounce) can chili with beans
1 (15-ounce) can golden hominy, drained
½ cup chopped onion
1 (2-ounce) can sliced ripe olives, drained, divided
1¼ cups shredded sharp Cheddar cheese

Stir together chili, hominy, onion, and ½ the olives. Pour in a lightly greased casserole dish and bake at 350° for 25 minutes. Cover with cheese, then remaining olives, and bake another 5 minutes. Serves 6.

Beer Beef Stew

1½ pounds stew meat
2 medium onions, chopped
8 ounces mushrooms, sliced
1 (12-ounce) can beer

Sauté meat and onions in large skillet; add mushrooms. Transfer to large baking dish. Pour beer in skillet and stir to scrape drippings; pour over meat in baking dish. Cook 3 hours at 325°. Serve over noodles or rice. Serves 6.

Editor's Extra: If you prefer thicker "juice," shake a tablespoon or two of flour in a jar with ⅓ cup hot water, and stir into stew.

Keep-The-Lid-On Stew Pot

2 pounds stew meat
1 package dry onion soup mix
1 (10¾-ounce) can cream of mushroom soup
1 (4-ounce) can mushrooms, drained
⅔ soup can water

Cut meat into bite-size pieces; put in large roasting pan with lid. Add soup mix, soup, mushrooms, and water; mix well. Cook, covered, at 300° for 3 hours. Do Not Peek! Keep the lid on! Serves 6.

Fab more taste

Crabmeat Stew Fit for a King

1 cup milk
2 cups heavy cream
1 pint pasteurized crabmeat
Salt, pepper, and cayenne to taste
½ stick butter

Heat milk and cream to boiling point; add crabmeat and bring back to boiling point. Season with salt, pepper, and cayenne to taste. Ladle into hot soup bowls containing a pat of butter in bottom. Garnish with parsley or paprika, if desired. Serves 4–5.

Editor's Extra: Good in puff pastry cups (the queen would love this for a luncheon), or over corn waffles or toast points.

More **Fast**
and
Fabulous

FIVE ★ STAR

Salads

Wilted Spinach with Tomatoes

1 bunch fresh baby spinach
3 Roma tomatoes
1–2 teaspoons bacon drippings, or butter
1 teaspoon Greek seasoning

Wash spinach well; dry on paper towels, remove stems. Slice tomatoes into wedges; set aside. In large skillet or saucepan melt bacon drippings. Toss spinach quickly in pan, tossing to coat and wilt. (It will wilt quickly.) Add tomatoes and sprinkle with seasoning. Toss several times to coat and slightly warm tomatoes. Serve immediately. Serves 4.

Spinach Salad with Seasonal Fruit

1 bunch fresh spinach, trimmed, washed, dried
3 cups fresh peeled, sliced peaches, nectarines,
**   pears, or strawberries**
1 cup shredded Swiss cheese
⅓ cup chopped walnuts
Poppy seed dressing

Mix spinach, fruit, cheese, and nuts in glass salad bowl. Just before serving, pour dressing over and toss thoroughly. Serves 6.

Caesar Salad with Steak Strips

1 (10-ounce) bag chopped romaine lettuce
2 tablespoons Caesar salad dressing
1 (7-ounce) package fajita steak strips, fully
**   cooked**
Croutons

Toss lettuce with dressing in large bowl. Divide greens evenly among 4 plates. Top each with ¼ of the steak strips. Season with black pepper, if desired, and top with croutons. Serves 4.

Homemade Croutons

A good way to make stale bread delicious!

Bread slices
Butter, softened
Parmesan cheese
Seasoned salt
Italian seasoning

Butter slices of bread. Sprinkle with Parmesan, then seasoned salt and Italian seasoning. Freeze slightly to make cutting easier. Cut into small cubes. Preheat oven to 350°. Place bread cubes in single layer in pan; put in oven; turn oven off, and leave overnight. Keeps a long time in an airtight container.

Quick Ham and Apple Salad

1 cup chopped cooked ham
2 hard-boiled eggs, chopped
4 tablespoons sweet pickle relish
1 tart apple, peeled, chopped
½ cup ranch dressing or mayonnaise

Combine ham, eggs, pickle relish, apple, and dressing or mayonnaise. Serve on lettuce or baby spinach leaves. Serves 4.

Curry Chicken Salad on Pineapple

1 pint prepared chicken salad
2 teaspoons curry powder
⅛ teaspoon cayenne pepper
8 fresh pineapple slices

Combine chicken salad, curry powder, and cayenne. Mix well. Arrange pineapple on 4 plates. Spoon equal amounts of salad on top of pineapple. Serves 4.

Editor's Extra: May add sliced grapes, green onions, or almonds, if desired.

Fastest Snake on Land

The aggressive black mamba found in the southern part of tropical Africa is the **fastest** snake on land. You might have heard stories about this snake overtaking people on galloping horses, but although these snakes are **fast**, they aren't that fast. They can reach top speeds of 10–12 mph in short bursts over level ground.

Fastest Horse

Since horse racing, and more important- ly, betting on horse racing began, breed- ers have been breed- ing horses to go **fast**. The result is the American Quarter Horse, the world's **fastest** horse, which can sprint at up to 55 mph.

Extraordinary Shrimp Salad

4 cups cooked, deveined shrimp
½ teaspoon curry powder
Juice of 1 lemon
1 cup pineapple tidbits, drained
1 cup finely diced celery

Combine shrimp with curry powder and lemon juice, and let sit awhile. Combine pineapple and celery and add to shrimp; toss lightly. May sprinkle with toasted sliced almonds, if desired. No dressing is necessary. Serves 4–6.

Tropical Seafood Salad

1 cup cooked crabmeat
1 rib celery, finely chopped
1 tablespoon lime juice
½ teaspoon coconut flavoring
2 tablespoons mayonnaise

Combine all ingredients; mix lightly. Serve on bed of lettuce, or in fruit cups. Serves 2–4.

Colorful Pepperoni Pasta Salad

1 (16-ounce) bag frozen broccoli, red peppers,
**   onions, and mushrooms**
2 cups cooked macaroni
1 (3-ounce) package thinly sliced pepperoni
⅔ cup ranch dressing

Cook vegetables according to package directions; drain. Combine vegetables with macaroni in large bowl. Chill. Toss with pepperoni and dressing. Salt and pepper to taste. Serves 4–6.

Dilly Pork 'n Bean Salad

So good for picnics and barbecues.

1 (16-ounce) can pork and beans, drained
2 hard-boiled eggs, chopped
2 tablespoons dill pickle relish
⅓ cup chopped onion
¼ cup mayonnaise

Combine all ingredients; chill an hour or more. Best when made a couple of days ahead. Serves 4.

Easy English Pea Salad

1 (10-ounce) package frozen English peas
½ cup raisins
½ cup chopped cashews
Mayonnaise to taste

Cook peas per package directions; drain. Let cool. Soften raisins in boiling water to cover; drain. Let cool. Combine peas, raisins, and cashews in serving bowl; mix well. Add enough mayonnaise to reach desired consistency. Serves 4.

Pretty Asparagus Salad

Bibb lettuce leaves
1 (15-ounce) can asparagus spears, drained
2 hard-boiled eggs, wedged
8 cherry tomatoes, halved
Mayonnaise or poppy seed dressing

Place lettuce leaves on 4 salad plates. Arrange asparagus spears in spoke fashion over lettuce with egg wedges in between. Place tomato halves to make center circle and place a dollop of mayonnaise in center. Serves 4.

Rice and Veggie Salad

¾ cup Italian dressing
¾ cup mayonnaise
1 (16-ounce) can Veg-All, drained
2 packages boil-in-bag rice, cooked

Mix dressing and mayonnaise; add vegetables and rice; toss well. Serve chilled. Serves 8.

Marinated Tomato Salad

6 medium tomatoes, diced
2 green bell peppers, diced
1 onion, diced
2 tablespoons sugar
2 tablespoons vinegar

Combine vegetables; sprinkle with sugar and salt and pepper to taste. Add vinegar and stir. Let sit 2 hours before serving. Serves 4.

Marinated Tomato Topper

Good all by itself, too. Prepare ahead of time, then have on hand to make a quick lettuce-and-tomato salad.

1 container cherry or grape tomatoes
1–2 tablespoons chopped fresh basil
(or 1 teaspoon dried)
⅓ cup seasoned rice wine vinegar

Cut tomatoes in half. Put in container with lid. Add basil and vinegar and toss to coat. Refrigerate, covered, at least one hour. Will keep for many days. Scoop over torn lettuce leaves on individual plates for ready-to-serve salads. Serve with assorted crackers. Serves 4–6.

Editor's Extra: You can pour over regular sliced tomatoes, too. Pretty with basil leaves as garnish.

A Salad of Marinated Onion Rings

This is so good with fish. Good with lettuce and tomatoes, too.

½ cup sugar
3 tablespoons vinegar
2 large onions, sliced in rings
¾–1 cup mayonnaise
1 tablespoon dry buttermilk ranch dressing (or
  celery salt)

Mix sugar and vinegar. Pour over onion rings in a flat-bottomed bowl or casserole dish; pour vinegar mixture over top. Add some water to cover. In separate bowl, mix mayonnaise and dressing; refrigerate both onions and dressing for a half hour.

When ready to serve, drain onions, then fold mayo dressing into onions. Serves 4–6.

Marinated Vidalia Onions

2 Vidalia onions, thickly sliced
1 cup sour cream
½ teaspoon salt
3 tablespoons sugar
3 tablespoons vinegar

Combine all ingredients. Keep chilled till serving time. Serves 4–6.

**Fastest Roller
Coaster in the USA**

Kingda Ka is a roller coaster located at Six Flags Great Adventure in New Jersey, claiming the title of **fastest** roller coaster in the USA from Top Thrill Dragster at Cedar Point in Ohio when it opened on May 20, 2005. The roller coaster is launched by a hydraulic launch mechanism to 128 mph in 3.5 seconds. At the end of the launch track, the train climbs the main top hat tower reaching a height of 456 feet.

Dressed-Up Cucumbers

When cucumbers are plentiful in my garden, I love fixing this simple salad. —Barbara Moseley

4 cups sliced cucumbers (peel, if you like)
1 cup mayonnaise
¼ cup vinegar
¼ cup sugar
½ teaspoon salt

Put cucumbers into glass bowl. Combine remaining ingredients and toss with cucumbers. Cover and refrigerate at least 2 hours. Serves 6–8.

Italian Potato Salad

10–12 new red potatoes, cooked, quartered
¼ cup chopped chives
¼ cup chopped ripe olives
¼ cup chopped parsley
½ cup Italian salad dressing

Combine hot potatoes, chives, olives, and parsley in bowl. Pour dressing over hot mixture; toss gently to coat. Refrigerate 1–2 hours. Toss again just before serving. Serves 8.

Great Beet Gelatin Salad

¼ cup sugar
1 (3-ounce) package lemon Jell-O
1 (16-ounce) can beets, reserve juice
1 (8-ounce) can crushed pineapple, reserve juice
1 cup chopped nuts (optional)

Mix sugar, Jell-O, and juices in a saucepan and bring to a boil, stirring to dissolve Jell-O. Mash beets and mix all together, mixing thoroughly. Refrigerate to gel. Serves 6–8.

Creamy Carrot Raisin Salad

3 cups peeled, grated carrots
¾ cup seedless raisins
1 teaspoon sugar
¼ cup mayonnaise
2 tablespoons cream cheese, softened

Combine carrots, raisins, and sugar. Mix remaining ingredients and stir into carrot mixture. Salt and pepper to taste. Chill before serving, if desired. Makes 6–8 servings.

Sun and Moon Salad

1 pound carrots, scraped, finely chopped
1 (8-ounce) can crushed pineapple, undrained
½ cup raisins
½ cup chopped nuts (optional)

Combine all ingredients; cover and refrigerate till serving time. Serves 4–6.

Curried Avocado Salad

16 (¼-inch-thick) slices avocado
16 (¼-inch-thick) slices tomato
Lemon juice
⅔ cup sour cream
1 teaspoon curry powder

Arrange avocado and tomato slices on 4 salad plates. Brush avocado slices with lemon juice. Mix sour cream and curry powder till smooth. Dollop over avocado and tomato slices. Serves 4.

Colorful Mandarin Avocado Salad

1 head red-tipped leaf lettuce
2 (11-ounce) cans Mandarin oranges, drained
2 avocados, peeled, cut in chunks
1 small red onion, thinly sliced, separated
Poppy seed dressing

Tear lettuce into bowl; add Mandarin oranges, avocados, and onion rings. Toss with poppy seed dressing before serving. Makes 8 servings.

Sunshine Orange Salad

Pretty to put a square on lettuce leaves with a dollop of whipped cream and a maraschino cherry.

2 (3-ounce) boxes orange gelatin
2 cups very hot water
1 (11-ounce) can Mandarin oranges, drained,
  reserve juice
1 (6-ounce) can frozen orange juice
  concentrate, thawed
1 cup ginger ale

Dissolve gelatin in hot water. Add reserved Mandarin juice, orange juice, and ginger ale. Chill till slightly thick, then fold in Mandarin oranges. Chill till firm in salad mold or serving dishes. Makes 8–10 servings.

Peach-Mandarin Salad

A tango in your mouth!

1 (3-ounce) package lemon gelatin
1 (3-ounce) package orange gelatin
1 (11-ounce) can Mandarin oranges, drained,
  reserve juice
1 (16-ounce) can spiced peaches, drained,
  pitted, mashed, reserve juice

Prepare gelatins together according to directions, using the juice from both fruits plus water for the required liquid. Add oranges and mashed peaches. Chill to partially thicken, then pour into oiled molds or pan. Chill till firm. Serve on lettuce leaves or other salad greens. Serves 4–6.

Peach Aspic

Interesting spice flavor.

1 (3-ounce) package lemon gelatin
1 cup hot water
1 (16-ounce) can sliced peaches, drained,
  reserve juice
½ cup (or less) chutney

Dissolve gelatin in water; mix with ¾ cup reserved peach syrup (add water if needed). Add peaches and chutney; chill till firm. Great on mixed greens. Serves 4–6.

Fastest Swim of the English Channel

6 hours, 57 minutes, and 50 seconds by Petar Stoychev (Bulgaria) from Shakespeare Beach, Dover, UK, to Cap Gris Nez, France on August 24, 2007.

Fastest by Waterski - 29 minutes and 26 seconds by Micha Robyn (Belgium) on May 24, 2007.

Fastest by a canoe/kayak - 2 hours and 59 minutes by Ian Wynne (UK) October 5, 2007.

Apricot Ring of Sunshine

2 (16-ounce) cans apricot halves, drained, reserve syrup
2 (3-ounce) packages orange Jell-O
1 (6-ounce) can frozen orange juice concentrate
2 tablespoons lemon juice
1 (7-ounce) bottle lemon-lime soda

Purée apricots. Bring reserved syrup to a boil; dissolve Jell-O in syrup. Add purée, orange juice, and lemon juice. Stir until orange juice is melted. Slowly pour soda down side of pan; stir well. Pour gelatin mixture into a 6½-cup ring mold. Chill until firm. Serves 6–8.

Strawberry Jell-O Surprise

2 (3-ounce) boxes strawberry Jell-O, divided
1 (16-ounce) package frozen strawberries, thawed, divided
1 (16-ounce) carton sour cream
1 cup chopped pecans

Prepare 1 box Jell-O per package directions in large serving dish; allow to set. Spread ½ the strawberries over firm Jell-O. Spread sour cream over strawberries. Spread remaining strawberries over sour cream. Prepare remaining box of Jell-O and pour mixture over strawberries. Sprinkle with pecans and refrigerate till firm. Serves 6–8.

Elegant Blueberry Layer Salad

Mold in a graham cracker or pretzel or chocolate crust for a great dessert.

1 (8-ounce) package cream cheese, softened
1 (3-ounce) package lemon Jell-O, dissolved in
  1¼ cups hot water
1 (8-ounce) carton whipped topping
2 (3-ounce) packages strawberry Jell-O
1 (12-ounce) package frozen blueberries

Mix cream cheese with dissolved lemon Jell-O; fold in whipped topping. Spread in 9x9-inch dish and refrigerate till firm. Dissolve strawberry Jell-O in 2½ cups hot water; chill till slightly thickened. Fold in frozen blueberries; pour mixture over cream cheese mixture and chill until ready to serve. Makes 9–12 squares.

Editor's Extra: May serve with a dollop of sour cream on top.

Frozen Cherry Salad Cups

1 (21-ounce) can cherry pie filling
1 (14-ounce) can sweetened condensed milk
1 (16-ounce) container Cool Whip
1 (15-ounce) can crushed pineapple, drained
1 (11-ounce) can Mandarin oranges, drained

Mix all ingredients gently but thoroughly in large bowl; pour into lightly sprayed 9x13-inch pan. Freeze, covered, 3 hours or more. Cut into squares to serve. Pretty on butter lettuce leaves. Serves 12.

I hope to stand firm enough to not go backward, and yet not go forward **fast** enough to wreck the country's cause.
—*Abraham Lincoln*

87

Throw Together Fruit Salad

1 (21-ounce) can cherry pie filling
1 (20-ounce) can pineapple chunks, drained
1 (11-ounce) can Mandarin oranges, drained
4 bananas, sliced
Chopped nuts or marshmallows (optional)

Combine all ingredients well. Chill in refrigerator. Serves 6–8.

Delightful Fruit Salad

3 navel oranges, peeled, sectioned, drained
3 pears, peeled, chopped big
1 red apple, peeled, chopped big
½ cup raisins
Poppy seed dressing

Mix fruits together in serving bowl. Just before serving, pour dressing over and toss to coat. Serves 10.

Editor's Extra: May sub mayo and/or sour cream for the poppy seed dressing.

Snappy Apple Salad

A winner . . . even kids like it.

5 Granny Smith apples, peeled, diced
1 (12-ounce) package brickle bits or Heath Bits
1 (8-ounce) carton frozen whipped topping
1 (3-ounce) package vanilla instant pudding mix

Stir apples, and brickle bits in bowl. Fold whipped topping with dry pudding mix; toss with apple/bits mixture. Refrigerate. Serves 6–8.

Frozen Cranberry Salad Cups

1 cup whipping cream
¼ cup sugar
2 tablespoons mayonnaise
1 (16-ounce) can whole cranberry sauce,
  broken up
½ (6-ounce) can frozen orange juice, thawed,
  undiluted

Whip cream to soft peaks; fold in sugar and mayonnaise. Carefully fold in cranberry sauce and orange juice. Put paper liners in muffin tins; fill with salad and freeze. To serve, remove from refrigerator about 10 minutes before serving. Remove from paper cups onto lettuce-lined salad plates. Needs no dressing. Serves 6–8.

Holiday Cranberry Salad

2 (3-ounce) packages strawberry Jell-O
2 cups boiling water
1 (16-ounce) can jellied cranberry sauce
1 cup sour cream

Dissolve Jell-O in water; chill till thickened. Process cranberry sauce and sour cream till smooth. Combine with Jell-O, and pour into 3-cup mold. Refrigerate till set. Serves 6–8.

Editor's Extra: May use whole cranberry sauce, if desired.

Frozen Thanksgiving Salad

1 (16-ounce) can whole-berry cranberry sauce
1 (8-ounce) can crushed pineapple, drained
1 (8-ounce) carton sour cream
½ cup chopped nuts

Combine all ingredients and pour into individual serving cups. Freeze overnight. Serves 8–10.

Pear Crumble Salad

2 ripe red Bartlett pears, sliced, pitted
1 tablespoon lemon juice
4 ounces blue cheese, crumbled
½ cup chopped pecans, toasted
½ cup Italian salad dressing

Place pears cut side up on chilled salad plate; sprinkle with lemon juice. Combine crumbled blue cheese and toasted pecans. Put ¼ of mixture in each pear half; drizzle with Italian dressing. Chill till ready to serve. Serves 4–6.

Editor's Extra: Line salad plate with lettuce, if desired.

More **Fast** and **Fabulous**

FIVE ★ STAR

Vegetables

Spiced-Up Sweet Potatoes

4 small sweet potatoes
1 (3-ounce) package cream cheese, softened
2 tablespoons butter, softened
2–3 tablespoons brown sugar
¼ teaspoon pumpkin pie spice

Microwave sweet potatoes on #7 power 10–13 minutes or till tender. Beat cream cheese, butter, brown sugar, and spice together. When potatoes are done, make a slit in each one and fluff slightly. Put a dollop of cream cheese mixture in each. Serves 4.

Twice Baked Sweet Potatoes

6 large sweet potatoes, baked
½ stick butter
½ cup brown sugar
1 (8-ounce) can crushed pineapple, drained
½ cup chopped pecans

Cut a 1-inch wedge, lengthwise from each potato. Carefully scoop out pulp. Mix potato pulp, butter, sugar, and pineapple; beat till fluffy. Stuff mixture into potato shells and sprinkle with pecans. Bake at 375° for 10–12 minutes. Serves 6.

Editor's Extra: Okay to use 2 (28-ounce) cans sweet potatoes and bake in buttered casserole dish.

Lazy Day Potatoes

4 potatoes, peeled, sliced
3 tablespoons dry onion soup mix
1 stick butter

In a medium buttered casserole dish, layer potatoes, salt and pepper to taste, onion soup mix, and butter slices. Cover and bake in 325° oven 1 hour, uncovering the last 10 minutes. Serves 4.

Micro Magic Potatoes

½ stick butter
½ teaspoon garlic salt
1 tablespoon parsley flakes
½ teaspoon Cajun seasoning
**4 medium potatoes, scrubbed, cut in small
   chunks**

Melt butter in glass baking dish in microwave. Stir in garlic salt, parsley, and seasoning. Add potatoes and stir to coat. Cover with wax paper; microwave on #7 power 12 minutes (or 9 minutes on HIGH) till tender. Stir once or twice. Makes 5–6 servings.

Instant Potato Bake

1 (7-ounce) package instant potatoes
1 pint sour cream
6 green onions, chopped
5 slices bacon, cooked, crumbled
1½ cups grated cheese

Prepare potatoes by directions; spoon into greased casserole. Spread sour cream on top; sprinkle with green onions and bacon; top with cheese. Bake at 350° for 20 minutes. Serves 8.

Bacon-Cheese-Potato Casserole

3 pounds red potatoes
6–8 slices bacon, fried, crumbled
1 cup shredded Cheddar cheese
Onion salt and pepper to taste
½–1 stick butter, sliced

Boil whole potatoes in salted water 20 minutes. Do not peel. When cool, slice and layer into greased 9x13-inch baking dish. Add bacon bits, cheese, and seasonings to each layer. Top with butter slices. Bake uncovered at 350° for 40–45 minutes. Serves 4–6.

Creamy O'Brien Casserole

Variations on this classic dish just keep on pleasing.

1 (28-ounce) package frozen O'Brien potatoes
½ cup grated onion
1 (10¾-ounce) can cream of potato soup
1 (8-ounce) package cream cheese, cubed
1 (8-ounce) package shredded Cheddar cheese

Mix all ingredients together. Place in greased casserole dish and bake at 350° for 40–45 minutes. Makes 6–8 servings.

Editor's Extra: Nice to sub cream of chicken or celery soup for potato soup, and sour cream for cream cheese.

Company Creamy Mashed Potatoes

Make these ahead and refrigerate before baking. Handy and so delicious.

1 (5-pound) bag potatoes, peeled, diced, boiled, drained
1 (8-ounce) package cream cheese, softened
1 (8-ounce) carton sour cream
1½ sticks butter, divided

Mix all ingredients except ½ stick butter in mixer until smooth. Put in large buttered baking dish. Season with salt and pepper to taste. Melt remaining ½ stick butter and pour over top. Bake at 350° about 20 minutes till hot. Serves 10–12.

Simply Great Real Mashed Potatoes

6–8 medium russet potatoes, peeled
1 stick butter, melted
⅔–1 cup warm half-and-half

Cook potatoes in lightly salted water till tender; drain. Mash potatoes with butter and half-and-half, adding a little at a time till desired consistency is reached. Season with salt and pepper to taste. Serves 6.

Editor's Extra: To spruce up the potatoes a bit, add mashed garlic, diced green chiles, sour cream, or shredded cheese.

Fastest Typist

As of 2005, writer Barbara Blackburn was the **fastest** English language typist in the world, according to *The Guinness Book of World Records*. Using the Dvorak Simplified Keyboard, she maintained 150 words per minute for 50 minutes, and 170 wpm for shorter periods. She was clocked at a peak speed of 212 wpm. Ironically Blackburn failed her QWERTY typing class in high school.

Fastest Electric Car

Designed and built by engineering students at Ohio State, and driven by Roger Schroer at the Bonneville Salt Flats on September 25, 2009, the Buckeye Bullet 2 achieved a maximum speed of 303.025 mph. They gave their hydrogen fuel cell streamliner a nickname of "La Jamais Contente" in tribute to the first vehicle to go **faster** than 60 mph in 1899.

Awesome Stuffed Potatoes

6 medium baking potatoes, baked
2 cups shredded Jack cheese, divided
1 cup chopped, cooked broccoli
1 cup chopped ham
⅔ cup sour cream

Cut top off each potato while hot. Scoop out pulp into mixing bowl, leaving thick shell. Beat pulp, then stir in 1½ cups cheese, broccoli, ham, and sour cream, with salt to taste. Fill potato shells with mixture. Place on baking sheet and bake in preheated 400° oven 15 minutes. Sprinkle with remaining ½ cup cheese and bake 5 minutes more. Serves 6.

Hot Roasted Garlic Potatoes

Better make plenty.

5 medium potatoes, unpeeled, cut into ¾-inch chunks
3 garlic cloves, peeled, sliced
2 tablespoons olive oil
1 teaspoon Tabasco
1 teaspoon salt

Toss all together till potatoes are evenly coated. Bake in roasting pan in 400° oven 30–40 minutes, or till tender, stirring once mid-cooking. Serves 4–6.

Easy Veggie-Topped Baked Spuds

2 cups frozen broccoli-carrot medley
1 (10¾-ounce) can cream of broccoli soup
½ cup shredded Cheddar cheese
4 large baked potatoes

Microwave veggies in glass bowl on HIGH 4 minutes; drain. Add soup and cheese; stir. Microwave on HIGH until cheese melts and mixture is heated through, about 2 minutes. Split hot potatoes in half and fluff with a fork. Top with soup mixture. Salt and pepper to taste. Serves 4.

Super-Duper Stuffed Potatoes

Classically simple . . . and good!

4 medium baking potatoes, baked
½ stick butter
1 cup sour cream
1 cup shredded Cheddar cheese
4 bacon strips, fried, crumbled

When potatoes are cool enough to handle, split lengthwise; scoop out pulp leaving a thin shell. Mix potato pulp with butter till fluffy; add sour cream, cheese, and bacon. Fill potato shells. Place in baking dish and bake 25–30 minutes at 350°. Serves 4–8.

Editor's Extra: Use low-fat ranch dressing all by itself on a baked potato for a low-cal potato treat. Try other dressings, too.

Baked Garlic-Butter Potatoes

This is an easy potato dish that cooks while the steaks are on the grill or the roast is in the oven.

4 large baking potatoes, peeled
6 tablespoons butter, melted
Garlic salt
Parsley
Paprika

Slice potatoes like French fries. Place in casserole and pour butter on top. Season to taste with remaining ingredients and toss to coat well. Bake at 375° for 30–40 minutes till done. Serves 4–6.

Crusty Potato Chunks

4 medium potatoes, peeled, cut into 1-inch chunks
1 package dry onion soup mix
2 tablespoons oil
¼ cup chopped fresh parsley or 1 tablespoon dried

Boil potato chunks in water to cover for 5 minutes; drain. Mix potatoes with onion soup mix and oil; toss to coat. Place in shallow baking pan. Bake uncovered at 400°, stirring occasionally, 20 minutes, till crusty. Garnish with chopped parsley. Makes 6–8 servings.

Jimmy's Bacon-Wrapped Spuds

These are crazy good. —Jimmy Lamb

Large red potatoes, peeled
Sliced bacon
Lemon pepper seasoning

Poke potatoes a few times with a fork. Wrap a slice of bacon or two around each one and set on piece of foil. (Bacon should stick to itself, but if not, affix with toothpicks.) Sprinkle with lots of lemon pepper. Wrap up well in foil with slight opening on top. Place on middle rack of oven with a baking pan underneath. Bake for approximately 1 hour 15 minutes. Serve with butter and sour cream, or additional toppings of your choice.

Crusty Skillet Homemade Hashbrowns

4 large russet potatoes, baked
½ stick butter

Cool baked potatoes; refrigerate. When cold, peel. Grate potatoes with large grater or use food processor with large grater disk.

Heat butter over medium-high heat in 10-inch skillet until bubbly. Press grated potatoes evenly into skillet. Do not stir or turn potatoes. Salt and pepper to taste. Cook 10–12 minutes till golden brown. Remove from heat; invert serving plate over skillet. Turn potatoes onto plate. Serves 4–6.

I watched the Indy 500, and I was thinking that if they left earlier they wouldn't have to go so **fast**.

—*Steven Wright*

Joyce's Hashbrown Cheese Cups

These are crispy on the outside and so delicious. Reheat them the next day and they are just as tasty. Oven over microwave is best. —Joyce Cox

4 cups frozen shredded hashbrowns, partially thawed
3 eggs
¼ cup milk
½ onion, chopped
2 cups shredded sharp Cheddar cheese

Spray 12 muffin cups with cooking spray. Mix all together well and fill cups almost full. Bake 35–40 minutes at 350° till golden brown.

Editor's Extra: Tasty to add bacon bits or tiny ham chunks. Or add a tad of chopped red, orange, yellow, or green bell pepper for a colorful and extra taste treat.

Nacho Taters for Two

1 large potato, peeled, sliced ¼ inch
¼ cup picante sauce, divided
1 tablespoon chopped green onion
2 tablespoons chopped green chiles
⅔ cup shredded Cheddar cheese

Place potato slices in a microwave-safe baking dish in one layer. Salt to taste; brush with half the picante sauce. Cover with wax paper; cook on HIGH 4–5 minutes till tender. Brush with remaining picante sauce; sprinkle with green onion, green chiles, and cheese. Microwave, covered, on HIGH 30–60 seconds, till cheese is melted. Serves 2.

Parr Potato Pancakes

These are simply great! —Elisbeth Anne Parr

2 cups grated potatoes
¼ cup milk
1 egg, well beaten
2 tablespoons flour
1 tablespoon minced onion

Soak potatoes in cold milk; drain. Mix potatoes together with egg and flour; salt and pepper to taste. Stir in minced onions. Drop by spoonfuls onto a hot greased frying pan and cook till golden brown on both sides. Makes 8–10.

Second Time Around Patties

2 cups leftover mashed potatoes
1 egg, beaten
Dash of Cajun seasoning
2–3 tablespoons butter

Combine potatoes and egg; mix well. Add a dash of Cajun seasoning. Form into palm-size patties. Heat butter in flat-bottomed skillet; fry potato patties on medium-high heat till golden brown on each side. Serves 4–6.

Classic Cottage-Fries

¼ cup oil or shortening
6 cups peeled potatoes, cut in small pieces
½ cup chopped onion

Heat shortening in large skillet 5 minutes on medi-um-high heat. Add potatoes; season with salt and pepper. Cover tightly and fry till potatoes are brown; turn and add onion; stir gently. Remove cover for last few minutes of cooking time to crisp potatoes. Serves 6–8.

Skillet Potato Chunks

16 small new potatoes, scrubbed, quartered
6 tablespoons butter
1 clove garlic, crushed
⅓ cup grated Parmesan
Paprika

Boil potatoes till tender; drain and dry. Melt butter in skillet, sauté potatoes in butter and garlic till golden brown. Sprinkle with Parmesan and paprika and toss to coat. Serves 6.

Red Potato Strips

1 stick butter, softened
1 package dry onion soup mix
6 large red potatoes, scrubbed, cut into
fat strips
Cracked black pepper

Stir butter and soup mix together and pour over potatoes. Put potatoes in a buttered casserole dish; pepper generously. Cover and bake at 350° for 50 minutes. Remove cover; bake another 10 minutes. Serves 8.

Pan-Fried Potato/Cabbage Patties

3 medium red potatoes, peeled, cubed
½ head cabbage, cut up
1 teaspoon Old Bay Seasoning
2 tablespoons bacon drippings

Boil potatoes; drain and mash. Cook cabbage in water to cover 15 minutes; drain. Mix potatoes and cabbage together with seasoning. Shape into patties. Fry in hot bacon drippings in skillet on medium heat, turning often, till crisp on both sides. Season to taste. Serves 6–8.

Fab more taste

Simply Stewed Cabbage

1 head cabbage, sliced
2 tablespoons bacon drippings
Salt and pepper to taste
2 teaspoons sugar

Boil cabbage in water till tender-crisp; drain. Place cabbage in large skillet with remaining ingredients. Cook over medium heat till wilted, then turn heat up a little and continue cooking till cabbage is beginning to color, not brown. Taste for seasoning; add more black pepper, if desired. Serves 6–8.

Editor's Extra: May add ½ onion, chopped, when placed in skillet, if desired.

Apple Glazed Carrots

2 cups baby carrots
¼ cup unsweetened apple juice
2 teaspoons Dijon mustard
¼ cup apple jelly

Boil carrots in apple juice in skillet. Cover and simmer 10 minutes, or till carrots are crisp-tender. Uncover and cook over medium-high heat till liquid evaporates. Lower heat; stir in mustard and jelly till jelly melts and carrots are glazed. Serves 4.

Fried Carrots? Yes!

Well, sort of.

4 slices bacon
1 pound fresh carrots, scraped, sliced
1 medium onion, chopped
½ teaspoon salt
¼ teaspoon pepper

Fry bacon in skillet until crisp; remove and set aside. Add carrots and onion to bacon fat; sprinkle with seasonings. Cover and cook slowly until just barely tender. Uncover and cook, turning occasionally, until carrots are slightly brown. Crumble bacon and add to carrots. Serves 6–8.

Marshmallow Vanilla Carrots

The marshmallows make a lovely glaze. The flavor is delicious!

2 (12-ounce) packages frozen petite carrots
2 tablespoons sugar
1 cup mini marshmallows
3 tablespoons butter
1 teaspoon vanilla

Boil carrots in water to cover till tender with sugar and salt and pepper to taste. Drain all but ½ cup liquid. Add remaining ingredients; gently stir till marshmallows melt. Serves 8–10.

Memory Lane Lima Beans

Like grandma used to make.

1 chunk country bacon or salt pork
1 (16-ounce) bag frozen lima beans
1 teaspoon sugar
1 cup milk mixed with 1 tablespoon flour
2 tablespoons butter

Boil bacon or pork in a cup or so of water till soft. Add beans and sugar. Add milk mixture to beans; add butter and stir gently. Salt and pepper to taste. Return to boil; cook on medium heat till beans are tender. Serves 4.

Lazy Day Oven-Baked Butterbeans

4 slices bacon
1 onion, chopped
1 cup sliced carrots
1 (16-ounce) package frozen butterbeans
1 teaspoon salt, or to taste

Brown bacon over medium heat with onion and carrots. Add to baking dish with butterbeans. Add salt to taste. Barely cover with water, and bake at 300° for 3 hours. Serves 4.

Gee Whiz Green Beans

1 (16-ounce) package frozen green beans
⅓ cup Cheez Whiz, divided
1 small onion, chopped
½ pound fresh mushrooms, sliced
1 tablespoon oil

Cook green beans according to package directions; drain. Stir in ½ of Cheez Whiz. Sauté onion and mushrooms in oil. Add beans and remaining ½ of Cheez Whiz. Serves 4.

Garlic Green Beans

1 pound fresh green beans, stemmed and snapped
2 tablespoons butter
1 teaspoon lemon juice
1 clove garlic, finely minced

Cook beans in a quart of boiling salted water 8 minutes, till tender. Drain, and rinse with cold water. Melt butter in skillet; add lemon juice and garlic. Stir in green beans and cook till heated through. Season to taste. Serves 4.

Southern Green Beans

⅓ cup vinegar
⅓–½ cup light brown sugar
2 tablespoons bacon grease
2 (15-ounce) cans whole green beans (reserve liquid from 1 can)

Simmer first 3 ingredients in large saucepan. Add liquid from 1 can of beans. Simmer. Add green beans; salt and pepper to taste. Stir gently so as not to break beans. Cover and simmer 20 minutes. Serves 4–6.

Fastest-Selling Book

In March 2008, the seventh and final volume in the Harry Potter series, *Harry Potter and the Deathly Hallows,* became the **fastest-selling** book in history, with more than 11 million copies sold during the first 24 hours.

Pepper Dill Beans

½ pound fresh green beans, stemmed
1 tablespoon butter
½ teaspoon cracked black pepper
1 teaspoon dill weed
1 teaspoon lemon juice

Steam beans till tender. Melt butter in large skillet; toss in beans. Sprinkle with pepper, dill weed, and lemon juice. Toss to coat beans. Serves 4.

That's All Broccoli

Fast, delicious, nutritious.

Fresh broccoli stems
Seasoned rice wine vinegar

Steam broccoli to desired tenderness. Place in serving dish or plates, and shake rice vinegar over, not too heavily. That's all!

Tasty Broccoli Casserole

1 bunch fresh broccoli spears, or 2 (16-ounce) packages frozen broccoli
1 (10¾-ounce) can cream of celery soup
1 (8-ounce) carton sour cream
Grated Parmesan or Romano cheese

Steam broccoli till tender. Place in baking dish. Mix soup and sour cream and spread over top. Sprinkle with cheese. Bake at 350° for 30 minutes. Serves 8.

Broccoli Delight

1 bunch fresh or frozen broccoli
½ cup mayonnaise
½ cup sour cream
½ teaspoon prepared mustard
½ teaspoon lemon juice

Boil broccoli 15 minutes or till tender in small amount of water. Salt to taste. Do not overcook. Mix remaining ingredients well and heat till warm. Serve over hot, well-drained broccoli. Serves 4.

Cheesy Cauliflower

1 head cauliflower, separated into florets
½ cup mayonnaise
2 tablespoons yellow mustard
1½ cups grated Cheddar cheese

Steam cauliflower till tender. Pour into greased casserole. Combine mayonnaise and mustard; spread on top; sprinkle with cheese. Bake uncovered for 30 minutes in 350° oven. Serves 4–6.

Fried Cauliflower Florets

1 head cauliflower
2 eggs, beaten
¼ cup milk
Seasoned flour

Cut cauliflower into florets. Dip cauliflower in egg-milk mixture and then into seasoned flour. Drop into hot (350°) oil and fry 2–3 minutes or till golden brown. Serves 4–6.

Batter Fried Eggplant

1 eggplant
1–2 eggs, beaten
½ cup seasoned Italian bread crumbs
½ cup fish fry (or flour)
⅓ cup oil

Peel and cut eggplant into thin slices; soak in salted water for 10 minutes. Drain well, then dip in egg; roll in mixture of crumbs and fish fry. Fry in hot oil in skillet till browned on both sides. Drain on paper towels. Serves 4.

Zing Squash

2 small yellow squash, sliced
1 medium zucchini, sliced
⅓ cup chopped red bell pepper
1 teaspoon Cajun seasoning
2 tablespoons olive oil

Sauté all in olive oil over medium heat while stirring, about 4 minutes; cover and turn off heat. Let sit covered till ready to serve. Makes 2–3 servings.

Super Skillet Squash

2–3 medium yellow squash, coarsely chopped
¼ stick butter, or 2 teaspoons bacon drippings
1 medium onion, chopped
1 teaspoon sugar
2 teaspoons Creole seasoning

Boil squash in water to cover till just tender; drain well. Melt butter in skillet; add onion, squash, sugar, and seasoning. Stir-fry over medium heat till onion is tender and squash starts to brown slightly. Serves 4–6.

Baked Squash Medley

3 yellow squash, chopped
¾ cup frozen vegetable seasoning blend
  (peppers, onions, celery)
1 egg white, beaten till stiff
½ cup mayonnaise
½ cup shredded Cheddar cheese

Cook squash in salted water to cover till tender; drain well. Add seasoning blend to squash and mix well. Fold egg white into mixture; pour into greased 9-inch pie plate. Combine mayonnaise and cheese. Cover top of squash mixture with cheese mixture. Bake in 350° oven 20–30 minutes till hot and bubbly. Serves 4.

Fastest Dog

The greyhound can reach speeds of up to 45 mph. This breed of dog can be traced back to ancient Egypt over 6,000 years ago. It was a revered dog, one that has been found engraved on caves throughout history. Today, it is mainly used for hunting and racing. The greyhound has long powerful legs, a broad chest, and is at its best when it is running.

The Best Squash Casserole

5 medium yellow squash, sliced
1 small onion, sliced
2 tablespoons butter or bacon fat
12 club crackers, divided

Boil squash and onion in water to cover till tender. Drain; add butter or bacon fat and salt and pepper to taste with 8 crackers, crumbled; mix well. Pour into greased casserole and sprinkle with remaining 4 crackers, crumbled. Bake 10 minutes in 400° oven. Serves 4.

Squash Fritters

2–3 yellow squash
1 onion, finely chopped
1 egg
1 cup cornmeal mix
Milk for consistency

Boil squash till tender; drain and mash. Sauté onion in a little butter or oil till tender; mix with squash. Add egg and cornmeal mix; combine thoroughly. Season to taste with black pepper, if desired. Add a little milk to mixture for consistency of cornbread batter. Fry by tablespoonfuls in hot oil till brown on both sides. Serves 4–6.

Parmesan Zucchini Boats

2 medium-size zucchini
¼ cup chopped onion
¼ cup chopped mushrooms
2 tablespoons olive oil
Parmesan cheese

Steam whole zucchini about 10 minutes, till just tender. Cut in half lengthwise; scoop out pulp; reserve. Sauté onion and mushrooms in oil till soft, about 2 minutes. Combine with reserved zucchini pulp; season to taste. Spoon mixture into zucchini halves (boats) and sprinkle with Parmesan cheese. Place in baking dish and bake 10 minutes at 350°. Serves 2.

Par Excellence Asparagus Casserole

An old favorite you can count on. —Elisbeth Anne Parr

2 (15-ounce) cans asparagus spears, drained
1 cup grated Cheddar cheese
1 (5-ounce) can evaporated milk
1 (10¾-ounce) can cream of mushroom soup
1 (3½-ounce) can French fried onions

Place asparagus in lightly greased casserole dish. Sprinkle cheese over asparagus. Mix milk and soup thoroughly and pour over cheese. Cook in 350° oven for 30 minutes. Then top with French fried onions, and continue to bake another 10 minutes. Serves 6–8.

Stir-Fried Asparagus

1 pound fresh asparagus, washed
2 tablespoons oil
2 tablespoons soy sauce

Snap off woody ends of asparagus and discard. Cut tender upper stems diagonally into 1-inch pieces. Season with salt and pepper to taste. Heat oil in skillet or wok. Add asparagus and cook, covered, over medium heat about 3 minutes, shaking pan from time to time. Remove from heat; stir in soy sauce and serve immediately. Serves 2–4.

Delicious Simply Fresh Asparagus

3 tablespoons olive oil
1 clove garlic, minced
1 bunch fresh asparagus, trimmed
¼ cup soy sauce
Toasted sesame seeds

Heat oil in skillet with garlic for about 3 minutes. Add asparagus spears, tossing gently. Sprinkle soy sauce over all. Cook 8–10 minutes, lightly browning on all sides. Sprinkle with sesame seeds and serve. Serves 4.

Asparagus à la King

Almost a meal in itself.

2 (16-ounce) cans asparagus spears, drained
2 (10½-ounce) cans Swanson's Chicken
  à la King
2 cups grated Cheddar cheese

Layer ingredients in order in a greased 9x13-inch casserole dish. Bake 20 minutes at 350° till cheese bubbles. Serves 6–8.

Editor's Extra: May substitute English peas with pearl onions for asparagus, if you prefer "Peas à la King."

Creamy, Crusty-Topped Asparagus

2 (10-ounce) cans cut asparagus, drained
1 (10¾-ounce) can cream of celery soup
¼ stick butter
½ cup shredded Cheddar cheese
1 (3-ounce) can French fried onions

In shallow baking dish, place asparagus; spread soup evenly over all. Place butter pats over soup; sprinkle with cheese; bake at 350° for 30 minutes, till hot and bubbly. Scatter onions over top and return to oven for 5 minutes. Serve immediately while onions are crispy. Serves 6.

Fastest Steam Locomotive

The London North Eastern Railway "Class A4" No. 4468 hauled seven passenger cars at a speed of 125 mph between Grantham, Lincolnshire, and Peterborough, Cambridgeshire, UK, on July 3, 1938.

Peas and Asparagus

A good combo.

1 (10¾-ounce) can cream of mushroom soup
1 (16-ounce) can tiny English peas, drained
1 (10-ounce) can asparagus, drained
1 (8½-ounce) can sliced water chestnuts, drained
¼ cup butter, melted

Pour soup in buttered casserole; pour peas over; arrange asparagus and water chestnuts; pour butter over all. Bake in 350° oven 30 minutes. Serves 6–8.

Swiss Green Pea Casserole

1 (8-ounce) carton sour cream
8 ounces grated Swiss cheese
3 (15-ounce) cans green peas and onions, drained
2 cups crushed cornflakes
¼ stick butter, melted

In saucepan, melt sour cream and Swiss cheese; stirring constantly. Add peas; mix well. Pour into sprayed 9x13-inch baking dish. Combine cornflakes and butter and sprinkle over pea mixture. Bake at 350° for 35 minutes. Serves 8–10.

Bacon-y Spinach Divine

1 (10-ounce) package frozen chopped spinach
1 (10¾-ounce) can cream of chicken soup
2 eggs, beaten
2 tablespoons bacon bits
¼ teaspoon garlic salt

Cook spinach according to package directions; chop finely. Combine soup, eggs, bacon bits, and garlic salt; mix well. Add spinach; mix well. Pour into greased 9-inch casserole dish. Bake at 325° for 30–35 minutes, or until hot and bubbly. Serves 4.

Granny's Creamed Spinach

1 (10-ounce) package frozen chopped spinach
½ (8-ounce) package cream cheese, softened
Pinch of nutmeg

Cook spinach per package directions. Drain well. Mix cream cheese, nutmeg, and salt and pepper with spinach till smooth. Bake in greased baking pan 10–12 minutes at 350°, uncovered. Serves 4.

Spinach Plus

1 (10-ounce) package frozen spinach
2 ounces low-fat cream cheese
⅓ cup grated sharp Cheddar cheese
1½ teaspoons Worcestershire

Cook spinach per package directions and add remaining ingredients while hot. Serve immediately. Serves 2–4.

Steamed Spinach with Garlic

Add a little zip to fresh spinach.

3–4 tablespoons olive oil
2 pods garlic, minced
1 bunch fresh baby spinach

Heat oil in large skillet; add garlic and simmer on low heat a few minutes; do not brown. Add spinach and toss well; add salt and pepper to taste, if desired. Cover and steam until spinach is tender. Serves 2.

Southern Turnip Greens

4 bunches turnip greens with turnips,
 washed well
6 slices bacon
2 teaspoons sugar

Remove turnips and stems from greens. Peel turnips and use only the young greens. Wash greens again, and tear into pieces. Cook greens in water to cover until tender, about 30 minutes. Peel and slice turnips; add to greens. Cook bacon, crumble, and add with drippings to greens. Cook about 15 minutes longer. Season to taste. Serves 6–8.

Tasty Quick Spinach

A delightful good-for-you veggie you can prepare in five minutes.

1 (10-ounce) package frozen chopped spinach
1 tablespoon butter
1 tablespoon Worcestershire
½ cup shredded Monterey Jack cheese

Microwave frozen spinach in covered dish 5 minutes, stirring once, till cooked. Stir in remaining ingredients. Serves 2–4.

Gruyère Baked Onions

These smell so good baking . . . and taste even better.

3 white onions
2 teaspoons olive oil (or butter)
⅔ cup beef broth
1 tablespoon teriyaki (or soy) sauce
⅔ cup finely shredded Gruyère cheese

Cut a small slice off top and bottom of onions, and remove outer peel. Cut in half (across), then set sliced side up in a greased casserole dish. Drizzle or brush onions with oil or butter; salt and pepper to taste. Bake in 400° oven 15 minutes. Mix broth and sauce and pour over each onion. Bake another 15 minutes. Sprinkle cheese on top and bake another 5 minutes or till cheese melts. Serves 3–6.

Editor's Extra: Almost any kind of cheese will do, especially Swiss, Parmesan, or feta.

Marinated Sweet Onions

Great as a side dish or on salads. —Mrs. Mary Farquhar

1 large onion, sliced thin
2 tablespoons white vinegar
¼ cup sugar
¼ cup plus 2 tablespoons vegetable oil

Mix all ingredients. Seal in an airtight container. Refrigerate overnight. Serves 2–4.

Fastest Doubleheader

The **fastest** double-header in Major League Baseball was played on September 26, 1926, between the New York Yankees and the St. Louis Browns, lasting only 2 hours and 7 minutes.

119

Micro-Baked Onions

Great with steaks on the grill.

1 large Vidalia onion, split crosswise
2 teaspoons butter, divided
½ teaspoon Greek seasoning, divided

Place onion halves side by side in microwave bowl. Place a teaspoon of butter on each half and sprinkle seasoning over each. Add about a tablespoon water to bottom of bowl; cover tightly; microwave 2–3 minutes.   Test for doneness by sticking a fork in onion. If not tender enough, microwave 1 minute more. Let stand till ready to serve; pour any juices over onion when serving. Serves 2.

Sweet Onion Pie

An easy brunch or lunch with fresh fruit alongside.

2 sweet onions, sliced
1 (9-inch) unbaked pie shell
2 eggs, beaten
¾ cup milk
1 cup grated Swiss cheese

Sauté onions in nonstick skillet till soft; pour into pie shell. Mix eggs, milk, and salt and pepper to taste; pour over onions. Sprinkle with grated cheese. Bake at 375° for 40–45 minutes. Serves 6.

Basil Baked Tomatoes

4 large fresh tomatoes
¾ cup bread crumbs
3 tablespoons chopped fresh basil
½ cup shredded Parmesan
3 tablespoons butter, melted

Slice tomatoes in half; cut stem indentions out. Combine bread crumbs, basil, and Parmesan. Stir melted butter into mixture till well mixed. Sprinkle mixture on top of tomato halves on lightly greased baking pan. Broil 5–8 minutes, till brown on top. Serves 8.

Okra and Tomato Magic

A southern treat that lots of Yankees like, too.

2 slices bacon, cooked, crumbled, reserve
  drippings
1 (14½-ounce) can chopped tomatoes
  with garlic
1 (10-ounce) package frozen cut okra
½ cup chopped onion
1 tablespoon Worcestershire

In saucepan combine bacon drippings, tomatoes, okra, and onion; cook over medium heat till tender. Add Worcestershire, bacon, and salt and pepper to taste; heat thoroughly. Serve over rice, if desired. Serves 6.

Fastest Draw

If you were transported back in time to the Wild West, you might want to take Howard Darby along, as he is the world's **fastest** draw. Darby accomplished the world record draw during the 2000 Canadian Champion-ships in Cochrane, Alberta, with a time of 0.252 seconds.

Southern Fried Okra

1 pound fresh okra
¾ cup buttermilk
1 cup flour
1 teaspoon baking powder

Slice okra in ½-inch pieces; salt and pepper to taste. Pour into flat-bottomed bowl and toss with buttermilk; let sit 30 minutes or so.

Mix flour with baking powder and a little extra salt and pepper; coat okra in mixture. Fry in hot oil till bronze. Drain on paper towels. Serves 4.

Tomato-Topped Corn Casserole

3 tablespoons butter
4–5 cups cut fresh corn
2 cups water
4 slices crisp-fried bacon, crumbled
2 large tomatoes, peeled, sliced

Sauté corn in butter in skillet about 5 minutes. Add water, bacon, and salt to taste; pour into buttered casserole dish. Arrange sliced tomatoes on top. Place in 350° oven and bake uncovered 30 minutes. Serves 5–6.

Editor's Extra: If using frozen corn kernels, use only 1½ cups water.

Western Corn Casserole

1 (15-ounce) can whole-kernel corn, drained
1 (15-ounce) can cream-style corn
1 (8-ounce) package cream cheese, cubed
1 (4-ounce) can green chiles, undrained
Bread crumbs, buttered

Combine corn and cream cheese in saucepan. Stir over medium heat till cheese melts. Stir in chiles. Pour into buttered casserole and scatter buttered bread crumbs on top. Bake at 325° for 15 minutes or till lightly browned. Serves 6–8.

Cheddar Corn Bake

2 (15-ounce) cans whole-kernel corn, drained
1½ cups frozen seasoning blend (chopped onion, pepper, celery)
3 eggs, beaten
1 cup shredded Cheddar cheese
2 teaspoons sugar

Mix ingredients together, adding salt and pepper to taste; pour into greased casserole dish. Bake at 350° for 40–50 minutes. Serves 6–8.

Perfect Purple Hull Peas

1 quart purple hull peas
1 large onion, diced

Wash peas; boil in water to cover with onion and salt and pepper to taste. Cover and simmer, stirring occasionally, for at least 1 hour till tender.

Editor's Extra: Serve with cornbread—great with the peas' potlikker poured over.

Fab more taste

Green Bean and Bacon Casserole

4 cups cooked green beans
8 slices bacon, crisp, crumbled
1 onion, chopped
½ cup sugar
½ cup vinegar

Layer half the beans, bacon, and onion in casserole dish; repeat ending with onion. In saucepan combine sugar and vinegar; bring to boil for 1 minute; pour over top. Bake in 325° oven 1½ hours. Serves 8–10.

Melinda's Hollandaise Sauce

4 tablespoons lemon juice
2 egg yolks
6 tablespoons butter, melted

In saucepan over medium-low heat, whisk lemon juice with egg yolks. Stir constantly over medium-low heat until sauce thickens and turns pale yellow. Remove from heat. If too thick, slowly whisk in hot water (1 tablespoon at a time) until desired consistency is reached.

More Fast and Fabulous

FIVE ★ STAR

Pasta, Rice, Etc.

Mini Bow Tie Toss

Ten minutes to yum!!! Serve with salad and bread for a fantastic quick meal.

½ (16-ounce) box mini farfalle pasta
2 (14½-ounce) cans diced tomatoes with basil, garlic, oregano, drained
1 (15-ounce) can whole-kernel corn, drained
1 teaspoon Greek seasoning
¼ cup shredded Parmesan cheese

Cook pasta in lightly salted boiling water for 7 minutes; drain. While pasta is boiling, heat tomatoes, corn, and seasoning in large saucepan. Toss with pasta and Parmesan cheese.

Editor's Extra: May substitute cut-up cooked chicken for corn, or use in addition to it.

Sweet Pepper and Basil Bow Ties

8 ounces red and yellow peppers, cut into strips
3 tablespoons olive oil
2 cloves garlic, chopped
4 leaves fresh basil, sliced
½ pound bow tie pasta, cooked

Sauté peppers in olive oil till slightly softened; add garlic. Cook 5 minutes; add basil and season to taste. Toss with pasta. Serves 6.

Spinach and Feta Pasta

1 (7-ounce) package angel hair pasta
1 tablespoon olive oil
1 (10-ounce) package frozen creamed spinach
1 (4-ounce) package shredded Parmesan cheese

Break pasta in half, and cook in boiling salted water for 7 minutes; drain; toss with olive oil. Microwave spinach according to package directions; toss in large serving bowl with cheese. Toss with hot pasta. Serves 4.

Pasta with Garlic Browned Butter and Fresh Parmesan

With a title like this, you expect it to be complicated. It's not!

6 tablespoons butter
1½ teaspoons minced garlic
8 ounces spaghetti, cooked, drained
½ cup freshly grated Parmesan cheese

In a small skillet, melt butter over medium-low heat. Add garlic and cook only till butter is light brown (watch carefully). Toss warm pasta with butter in large pot or bowl; put on individual serving dishes and sprinkle with fresh Parmesan cheese. Serves 4.

Speedy Gonzales

"The **Fastest** Mouse in all Mexico," is an animated cartoon mouse from the Warner Brother's *Looney Tunes* and *Merrie Melodies* series of cartoons. Speedy's major traits are his ability to run extremely **fast**, and his comedic Mexican accent. He usually wears an oversized yellow sombrero, white shirt and trousers, and a red kerchief. To date, there have been 46 cartoons made either starring or featuring this character.

127

Creamy Alfredo Sauce

You can serve this over meat, vegetables, or pasta. Also good as a snack with a toasted baguette. —Courtney Jernigan

1 teaspoon minced garlic
3 tablespoons butter
1 cup milk
1 cup shredded fresh Parmesan cheese
Pinch of flour (optional)

Sauté garlic in butter over very low heat 10–12 minutes. Add milk; cook and stir over medium-low heat till heated. Add Parmesan cheese and stir until cheese is melted and sauce has thickened slightly. If needed, add a pinch of flour to help thicken. It will continue to thicken as it cools. Serve over meat, vegetables, or pasta. Also good as a snack with a toasted baguette. Makes 2 cups.

Sausage Fettuccine

1 (8-ounce) package fettuccine
1 pound Italian sausage, skin removed, sliced
1 (10¾-ounce) can cream of chicken soup
1 (16-ounce) carton sour cream

Cook fettuccine; drain. Brown sausage about 8 minutes; drain on paper towels. Mix all ingredients; pour into greased casserole dish. Bake at 350° for 20–25 minutes. Serves 4–6.

Ratatouille Spaghetti Sauce

3 medium eggplants, peeled, diced
1/2 (16-ounce) package frozen pepper and onion blend
1 (14 1/2-ounce) can stewed tomatoes with celery, onion, green pepper
1 (14 1/2-ounce) can zucchini with Italian-style tomato sauce
3 1/2 jars roasted red peppers (optional)

Cook eggplants in water till tender; drain. Sweat pepper and onions in Dutch oven till tender. Add tomatoes, zucchini, red peppers, if desired, and eggplant. Add salt, pepper, and garlic salt, if desired. Cook over medium heat 20–25 minutes till flavors are well blended. Serve over hot pasta. Serves 8–10.

Zucchini and Mushrooms Baked in Spaghetti Sauce

A nice alternative to meat and pasta.

3 cups cubed zucchini
2 (4-ounce) cans sliced mushrooms, drained
1 (24-ounce) jar spaghetti sauce
1/2 cup freshly grated Parmesan cheese

Boil zucchini in small amount of water till barely tender; drain. Pour mushrooms into a greased casserole dish; add zucchini; pour sauce over. Bake in 400° oven 15–20 minutes till hot. Sprinkle cheese all over top. Bake till cheese is browned, about 5 minutes. Serves 6.

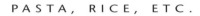

Corny Ravioli

2 (9-ounce) packages refrigerated cheese ravioli
1 tablespoon minced garlic
2 tablespoons olive oil or butter
2 cups frozen, thawed whole-kernel corn,
** or 1 (15-ounce) can, drained**
1 (14-ounce) can diced or stewed Italian-style
** tomatoes**

Cook ravioli per package directions and drain. Sauté garlic in oil or butter in skillet; add corn; cook and stir about 5 minutes. Add tomatoes and cook till hot. Season with pepper. Serves 6–8.

Editor's Extra: You may use a chopped fresh tomato instead of the canned, and add some Italian seasoning. Even more Italian with Parmesan sprinkled on top.

Everybody-Loves-It Casserole

1 pound ground chuck
1 (28-ounce) jar spaghetti sauce
1 (8-ounce) package small elbow macaroni,
** cooked, drained**
1½ cups grated mozzarella cheese, divided
1 (3-ounce) can grated Parmesan cheese

In large skillet, brown beef; drain; add spaghetti sauce, and when hot, add macaroni. Stir in ½ cup mozzarella and all the Parmesan. Pour into 2-quart greased baking dish. Sprinkle with remaining 1 cup mozzarella. Brown under broiler a few minutes till cheese melts. Serves 6–8.

Tuna Noodle Casserole

1 (7-ounce) package medium egg noodles
1 (15-ounce) can green peas, drained
2 (6-ounce) cans tuna, drained
2 (10¾-ounce) cans cream of mushroom soup

Cook noodles in boiling salted water for 3 minutes, stirring constantly. Cover and remove from heat. Layer drained noodles in well-greased casserole in with peas, tuna, and soup. If more liquid is needed, add a little milk. Bake 20–30 minutes. Serves 6–8.

Editor's Extra: May top with shredded cheese before baking, if desired.

What does a snail say when riding on a turtle's back?

Weeeeeeeeeeeeeee!

'Roni' Skillet Casserole

1 (7½-ounce) box macaroni and cheese
1 (5-ounce) package frozen meatballs
1 (10¾-ounce) can Cheddar cheese soup
1 (14½-ounce) can diced tomatoes
1 (15-ounce) can ranch-style beans, drained

Boil macaroni 7 minutes; drain. Set aside. In large skillet, brown meatballs; add cheese soup and cheese from macaroni package. Stir, then add tomatoes, cooked macaroni, and beans. Simmer 20–25 minutes. Serves 8–10.

Editor's Extra: Good to sub 1 pound ground beef for meatballs.

Dressed-Up Mac and Cheese

1 (7¼-ounce) box macaroni and cheese mix
1 (1.6-ounce) package McCormick's Zesty Herb Seasoning Mix
1 cup shredded Colby-Jack cheese

Make mac and cheese according to package directions. Stir in seasoning mix and put in a baking dish. Add cheese on top and bake in 350° oven for 5–8 minutes till cheese is melted. Serves 4–6.

Editor's Extra: May sub Mesquite or Tomato Garlic Basil seasoning mix, or mix of your choice. The possibilities are numerous.

Double Cheese and Macaroni

2 cups sour cream
2 (4-ounce) cans chopped green chiles, drained
3 cups raw elbow macaroni, cooked
¾ pound Monterey Jack cheese, cut into strips
½ cup grated Cheddar cheese

Combine sour cream, green chiles, and salt and pepper to taste. Butter a 2½-quart casserole dish. Put a layer of cooked macaroni on bottom, then a layer of sour cream mixture and a layer of cheese strips. Continue to layer (2 or 3) ending with macaroni on top. Cover and bake in 350° oven 20–30 minutes until hot and bubbly. Add grated Cheddar, and run back in oven till melted. Serves 8.

Alfredo Mac and Peas

2½ cups small macaroni
1 (16-ounce) jar Alfredo sauce
1 cup frozen baby peas
⅔ cup soft bread crumbs
3 tablespoons melted butter

Cook macaroni per package directions; drain and return to pot. Add Alfredo sauce and peas; cook over low heat, stirring until well combined. Pour into greased casserole dish, then top with the combined soft bread crumbs and melted butter. Bake at 350° about 25 minutes, until casserole bubbles and bread crumbs are browned. Serves 6.

Enchilada Express

1 (9-ounce) package regular-size corn chips
1 cup chopped onion
1 (16-ounce) can chili without beans
1 (8-ounce) package Mexican blend shredded cheese

Put chips in a large greased casserole dish; top with onion and chili. Cover with cheese. Bake at 375° for 15–20 minutes, or till cheese is melted. Serves 4.

Real Rice Pilaf

Not from a package, it's the real deal.

4 tablespoons butter
½ cup broken small vermicelli
1 cup long-grain rice
2 cups chicken broth

Melt butter in large skillet. Add broken noodles and rice; stir and cook till lightly browned. Add broth; season to taste with salt and pepper or seasoning of choice. Put in casserole dish and bake at 350° for 30 minutes. Fluff rice with fork before serving. Makes 4–6 servings.

Quickie Red Beans and Rice

6 strips bacon
1 cup minced onion
1 (15-ounce) can red beans, undrained
½ pound link sausage, casing removed, sliced
  (optional)
2 cups cooked rice

Fry bacon till crisp; set aside; reserve drippings. Sauté onion in drippings till tender. Add beans and simmer 30 minutes, covered, stirring occasionally. Fry sausage slices and add to bean mixture, if desired. May need to add a little water, if cooking too fast. Add rice, cover, and cook till heated through. Serves 6–8.

French Onion Rice

1 cup Uncle Ben's long-grain rice
1 (8-ounce) can sliced mushrooms, undrained
1 (10¾-ounce) can French onion soup
1 (8-ounce) can sliced water chestnuts, drained
6 tablespoons butter

Mix all ingredients except butter in greased casserole dish. Cover with pats of butter; bake uncovered at 350° for 1 hour. Serves 4–6.

Crawfish Rice Casserole

Easy and good!

1 (12-ounce) package frozen crawfish tails
**½ (12-ounce) package frozen seasoning blend
   (peppers, onions, celery)**
2 cloves garlic, minced
3 tablespoons butter
1 (7-ounce) package Spanish Rice-a-Roni

Sauté crawfish, seasoning blend, and garlic in butter till crawfish are just done. Prepare Rice-a-Roni by package directions; stir in crawfish mixture. Season to taste. Serves 6.

Editor's Extra: Fun to try other flavors of packaged rice mixes.

I don't think you realize just how **fast** you go until you stop for a minute and realize just how loud and how hectic your life is, and how easily distracted you can get.
—*Meg Ryan*

Green Chile Rice

1 cup raw rice, cooked per package directions
2 tablespoons butter
1½ cups sour cream
1 (4-ounce) can chopped green chiles
1 cup shredded Cheddar cheese, divided

Mix hot rice with butter; salt and pepper to taste; set aside. Combine sour cream and chiles. In a buttered casserole dish, put a layer of rice then a layer of chile mixture. Sprinkle ½ the cheese over top; repeat layers, topping with cheese. Bake at 350° for 20–25 minutes. Serves 6–8.

Nice Rice Casserole

1⅓ cups rice, uncooked
2 (10½-ounce) cans beef consommé
1 (4-ounce) can mushrooms, drained
1 medium onion, chopped
1 stick butter

Mix rice, consommé, mushrooms, and onion in a lightly greased 2-quart casserole. Slice butter over top. Cover; bake at 400° for 45 minutes, or till liquid is absorbed. Serves 6.

Baked Rice with Peppers

4 cups cooked rice
1 (4-ounce) can diced jalapeño peppers (or green chiles)
2 cups sour cream
1 cup grated Cheddar cheese

Combine rice, peppers, and sour cream in greased baking dish. Top with cheese; bake in 350° oven for 20 minutes, or until heated through. Serves 4.

Curry and Raisin Rice

This is really nice as a different side dish . . . and GOOD!

2 cups water
1 cup long-grain white rice
1½ teaspoons curry powder
2–3 tablespoons butter
⅓ cup raisins

Bring water with about a teaspoon of salt to a boil and stir in all ingredients. Cover and simmer about 18 minutes, till rice is cooked (or bake in casserole at 350° for about 40 minutes). Serves 6 or more.

Editor's Extra: When serving, add selected curry condiments of chutney, coconut, chopped peanuts, red bell pepper, and/or cilantro for a complete curry entrée.

Make-Your-Own Dumplings

4 eggs
1 teaspoon salt
3–4 cups all-purpose flour
1 (32-ounce) carton chicken broth
2 tablespoons butter

Beat eggs with salt. Add flour gradually till the texture of biscuits. Roll out thinly on floured surface, and cut into narrow strips. Boil chicken broth in large saucepan, then drop strips in a few at a time. Add butter and stir. Cook 30 minutes till tender. Serves 6–8.

Editor's Extra: Cook cut-up boneless chicken tenders in the broth, and you have some mighty fine chicken 'n dumplings.

Buffalo Pizza

1 (8-ounce) package cream cheese, softened
1 prepared (12-inch) pizza crust
1 cup blue cheese salad dressing
½ bag Boneless Buffalo Chicken Wings (I used Tyson AnyTizers), sliced
2 cups shredded mozzarella cheese

Spread softened cream cheese on pizza crust. Top with blue cheese dressing. Scatter Buffalo Chicken slices over top of blue cheese dressing. Top with mozzarella cheese. Bake at 375° for 15–20 minutes, or until cheese melts and barely begins to brown. Serves 8.

Cheezy Bones Pizza

*"I'll eat the bones," my son, Jules, would say of the edges of pizza slices because they are often left on the plate. But these "bones" are cheese filled, and so tasty, there won't be any left.
—Gwen McKee*

1 (13.8-ounce) can refrigerated pizza dough
7 (1-ounce) sticks string cheese
½ cup pizza sauce
1 (3.5-ounce) package sliced pepperoni
1 (8-ounce) bag shredded pizza-blend cheese

Place pizza dough in sprayed 12-inch pizza pan. Press dough outward from center to lap over edge by an inch. Place string cheese end to end all around pizza, then lap extended dough up over, pinching to seal. Bake in 425° oven 9 minutes till crust edge is bronze. Take from oven and pour sauce over crust evenly. Place pepperoni all around; sprinkle cheese over. Bake another 13 or more minutes till done. Serves 6–8.

Editor's Extra: "Bones" are especially good dipped in pizza sauce.

More Fast and Fabulous

FIVE ★ STAR

Meats

Spicy Good Meatloaf

1½ pounds lean ground beef
¾ cup Ritz Cracker crumbs
1 tablespoon Mrs. Dash Extra Spicy Seasoning
2 eggs
1 (8-ounce) can tomato sauce, divided

Heat oven to 350°. Mix beef, cracker crumbs, Mrs. Dash seasoning, eggs, ½ of the tomato sauce, and salt to taste. Put in loaf pan. Pour remaining tomato sauce over top. Bake 1 hour at 350°. Serves 6.

Wrap 'n Bake Dinner

½–¾ pound ground beef
2 red potatoes, peeled, sliced
1 carrot, sliced thin
1 onion, sliced

Make 4 patties with ground beef. On 4 pieces of heavy-duty foil, place patty and top with slice of potato, carrot, and onion; season to taste. Close foil tightly, folding edges together. Bake in 350° oven for 45–60 minutes. Serves 4.

Crazy Kraut Casserole

1 (16-ounce) can sauerkraut, undrained
1 cup minute rice
1 pound ground beef, browned, drained
1 (10¾-ounce) can tomato soup
1 (10¾-ounce) can chicken noodle soup

In 9x13-inch dish, layer ingredients in order listed. Do not stir. Bake at 350° for 1 hour. Serves 6–8.

Hamburger Steak and Gravy

A hands-down favorite.

1 pound ground chuck
1 envelope dry onion soup mix
½ cup all-purpose flour
1 tablespoon vegetable oil
1 envelope au jus gravy mix

Mix ground chuck and soup mix well; form into 4 patties. Combine flour with salt and pepper to taste; pat into meat patties. Brown steaks in oil in oven-proof skillet. Mix au jus as directed on package; pour over steaks and place in 350° oven. Bake 25–30 minutes, or till steaks are tender and gravy is thickened. Good with rice. Serves 4.

Stuffed Burger Bundles

1 pound ground chuck
¼ cup evaporated milk
1 cup herb stuffing mix, prepared
1 (10¾-ounce) can golden mushroom soup

Combine meat and milk with salt and pepper to taste; mix well. Divide into 4 or 5 patties. Put stuffing in center of patty and mold around it to form a ball. Put balls in greased 8x8-inch baking pan and pour soup over. Bake at 350° for 1 hour, basting often. Serves 4.

Sassy Burgers

1 pound lean ground beef
1 egg, beaten
1 tablespoon chili sauce
1 teaspoon seasoned salt
4 buns

Mix beef, egg, chili sauce, and salt well; form into 4 patties. Grill over medium heat 5–7 minutes each side, or till juices run clear. Serve on buns with your favorite toppings. Serves 4.

Southwest Hamburgers

4 hamburger patties
4 buns
4 slices pepper Jack cheese
1 avocado, peeled, thinly sliced
½ cup salsa

Grill patties over medium heat 5–7 minutes each side. Place patty on bottom of each bun; top with cheese while hot. Place avocado slices and salsa on top of cheese and replace top bun. Serves 4.

Dude Ranch Cheeseburgers

Thick or thin, these are dude-delicious.

1 (1-ounce) package ranch dressing mix
1 pound lean ground beef
1 cup shredded Cheddar cheese
1 (3½-ounce) can French fried onions
4–6 hamburger buns

Combine first 4 ingredients; shape into 4–6 patties; grill or pan-fry till no longer pink. Serve on toasted buns. Serves 4–6.

Beef and Bean Pot

2–3 pounds ground beef
1 onion, chopped
1 tablespoon margarine
2 (15-ounce) cans chili beans

In large skillet, brown beef and onion in margarine. Add beans and cook slowly 15–20 minutes, covered. Serves 8.

Pork 'n Beans to the N^(th) Degree

Kids love this and it's so easy to make!

1 pound ground beef
3 (15-ounce) cans pork and beans
1 package dry onion soup mix

Brown ground beef; drain. Add pork and beans and soup mix. Heat in 350° oven for about 20 minutes, until heated through. Serves 4–6.

Fastest Sportscar

In July 2006 at the British International Motor Show, Barabus Sportscars Limited unveiled the Barabus TKR, a V8 twin turbo, 1005 horsepower speedster that can do 0–60 mph in 1.67 and has a top speed of a blazing 270 mph. Buying one will result in the world's **fastest** lightening of your wallet by $689,138.74 if you bought it today.

Fab

Big-On-Taste Beef Tenderloin

1 (1½-pound) whole beef tenderloin
1 (8-ounce) bottle Italian dressing
4 garlic cloves, slivered
4 slices bacon

Pour dressing over tenderloin; marinate in refrigerator a few hours or overnight. Sear beef on all sides over medium heat. Remove to plate. Place garlic slivers in slit you make with a sharp knife. Wrap bacon slices around width of beef. Place on rack in shallow roasting pan. Roast uncovered at 375° to desired doneness. Serves 4–6.

Italian Beef

1 (5-pound) chuck roast
2 teaspoons minced garlic
3 teaspoons Italian seasoning, divided
2 cups water
½ cup red wine

Cover meat with garlic and about 2 teaspoons Italian seasoning. Place in roasting pan in 350° oven; roast about 1½ hours. Let cool; slice paper thin.

Add water and wine to pan drippings and sprinkle with remaining Italian seasoning. Add sliced roast to liquid and simmer till tender, about 1 hour. Serve with hard rolls. Serves 10–12.

Rump Roast au Jus

1 (3-pound) rump or sirloin tip roast
1 large onion, sliced
1 teaspoon garlic pepper
1 (14-ounce) can beef broth
1 (1-ounce) envelope au jus gravy mix

Brown roast on all sides in skillet. Place onion slices in bottom of crockpot and place roast on top; sprinkle garlic pepper all over; pat to adhere. Mix beef broth with au jus mix and pour over roast. Cover and cook on LOW for 6–8 hours or till tender. Remove roast and let sit about 10 minutes before slicing. Return slices to gravy and onion. Great served over rice or on hoagie buns. Serves 10–12.

My Favorite Pot Roast

The secret to any good pot roast is finding a really good cut of roast, one with plenty of marbling. —Barbara Moseley

1 (3- to 4-pound) chuck, 7-bone, or pot roast
1 envelope dry onion soup mix
½ cup water
1 (16-ounce) package frozen stew vegetables

Brown roast on both sides. Place in roasting pan with dry soup mix on top; sprinkle a little water over, then pour remainder in pot. Season with salt and lots of black pepper. Cook, covered, in 325° oven 1½ hours. Remove from oven and place frozen vegetables around roast in pot. Push down into liquid in pot. Cover and put back in oven another 30 minutes, or until vegetables are tender. Serves 6.

Editor's Extra: If you want your gravy a little thicker, remove roast and vegetables to platter and add a mixture of cornstarch and water to gravy. Cook on top of stove till as thick as you like.

2-Minutes-2-Fix Pot Roast

1 (3-pound) pot roast
1 tablespoon Worcestershire
1 package onion soup mix

In roasting pan, cover roast with Worcestershire and onion soup mix. Cover with foil and bake 3 hours at 300°. Serves 6.

Crockpot Barbecued Pot Roast

1 (2- to 3-pound) beef chuck roast
2 tablespoons oil
1 onion, chopped
⅔ cup barbecue sauce

Sear roast in hot oil on all sides in skillet, then transfer to crockpot. Add onion and barbecue sauce. Cover and cook on HIGH 4–5 hours, or on LOW 7–8 hours. Remove from pot; slice and serve with sauce. Serves 6–8.

Peppery Seared Rib-Eye Steak

Having your fire hot is the secret to a perfect steak; it seals in the juices.

4 (2-inch-thick) rib-eye steaks
2½ teaspoons hot sauce
Freshly ground black pepper

Rub steaks with hot sauce and pepper on both sides. Grill over hot fire about 5 minutes on each side. Salt to taste.

Tasty Teriyaki Steak

2 tablespoons sesame oil
1 teaspoon minced garlic
2 tablespoons brown sugar
1 tablespoon crushed fresh ginger
2 pounds top sirloin steak, cut into 4 pieces

Make marinade of first 4 ingredients; marinate steak in refrigerator overnight. Broil to desired doneness, turning once. May be cooked on outside grill also. Serve over hot rice. Serves 4.

Did you know that hair grows **faster** in summer than in winter, and **faster** during the day than at night?

Yacht Club Steak

Beautiful and delicious.

4 (8-ounce) filet mignons
8 tablespoons lump crabmeat
2 tablespoons butter
8 fresh asparagus spears, steamed
8 tablespoons hollandaise sauce

Grill or broil steaks to preferred doneness. Sauté crabmeat lightly in butter. Criss-cross 2 asparagus spears over each steak; drizzle with warm hollandaise; top with crabmeat. Serves 4.

Easy Beef Burgundy

1 (3-pound) round steak, cut in bite-size pieces
1 envelope mushroom onion soup mix
2 (10¾-ounce) cans cream of mushroom soup
¾ cup burgundy wine
½ teaspoon pepper

Coat steak in onion soup mix and put in 9x13-inch baking dish. Blend soup and burgundy, and pour over meat. Season with pepper. Bake, covered, 3 hours at 350°. Serve over rice. Serves 8–10.

In 1990, the *Guinness Book of World Records* declared Howard Stephen Berg "The **Fastest** Reader in the World." On Cleveland's "Morning Exchange," Howard completed an 1,100-page book and scored a perfect score on recall. He was retested three years later on the same book from the previous show, again with perfect recall.

Steak and Veggies in Stewed Tomatoes

4–5 potatoes, peeled, quartered
6–8 carrots, scrapped, sliced large
1 (2-pound) round steak
1 (14½-ounce) can Italian stewed tomatoes

Place potatoes and carrots in crockpot; sprinkle with salt and pepper to taste. Cut steak into serving pieces and lay on top of vegetables. Pour tomatoes over all. Cook on LOW about 8 hours, or until meat falls apart. Serves 4–6.

Steak and Mushroom Stroganoff

1½–2 pounds round steak
2 medium onions, chopped
1 stick butter
½ pound mushrooms, sliced
1 cup sour cream

Cut steak into ¼x2-inch strips; season to taste with salt and pepper. Brown meat and onions in butter; cook covered about 30 minutes. Stir in mushrooms and cook 10 minutes. Add sour cream and cook on low heat 10 minutes. Serve over rice, noodles, or angel hair pasta. Serves 4.

Beef Tips and Mushrooms

2 (10¾-ounce) cans cream of mushroom soup
1 envelope dry onion soup mix
1 cup red wine
2 pounds beef tips
2 cups mushrooms

Combine soup, soup mix, and wine in bowl; mix well. Add beef tips and mushrooms. Pour into 2-quart baking dish; bake, covered, at 350° for 2 hours. Remove cover and continue to bake 30 minutes longer. Serve over rice, if desired. Serves 4–6.

Zesty Grilled Flank Steak

1½ pounds flank steak
Seasoned meat tenderizer
Lemon pepper
½ bottle zesty Italian dressing

Sprinkle steak with tenderizer and lemon pepper; pour dressing over steak and refrigerate 3–4 hours before grilling. Cook until medium done and slice very thin at an angle across grain. Serves 4.

Marvelous Sautéed Mushrooms

Great on steaks, hamburgers, brisket . . . any kind of meat.
My dear friend Jeanne Turner made these and I wanted to
grab a fork and put the whole bowl in front of me.
—Gwen McKee

1 quart fresh mushrooms
½ stick real butter
2 tablespoons Worcestershire

Trim stems and slice mushrooms. Melt butter in a large skillet; add Worcestershire and mushrooms. Toss well to make sure all slices are coated. DO NOT SALT! Cover and cook on very low heat, stirring occasionally, at least one hour.

Wine-Sauced Brisket

1 (4-pound) beef brisket
1–2 envelopes dry onion soup mix
1 cup chopped onions
1 cup sliced mushrooms
2 cups red wine

Place brisket in baking dish. Sprinkle onion soup mix over and around brisket. Add onions, mushrooms, and wine. Bake at 250° for 4 hours. Baste occasionally. Serves 8–10.

Smothered Corned Beef

1 (4- to 5-pound) corned beef brisket
4 large potatoes, peeled, quartered
5 carrots, peeled, halved
1 head cabbage, quartered

Place corned beef in roaster; cover with water. Bring to a boil; turn heat down and simmer 3 hours. Add potatoes and carrots; place cabbage wedges over top of potatoes, carrots, and brisket. Salt and pepper vegetables. Bring to a boil; turn down and cook another 30–40 minutes, till vegetables are done. Slice corned beef across the grain. Serves 8.

less time

Fast

&

Smoky Pulled Pork

Great for burritos or pulled-pork buns.

1 (3-pound) pork butt roast
2 teaspoons liquid smoke
2 tablespoons rock salt
2 cups water

Rub roast with liquid smoke. Press rock salt into meat. Place in a Dutch oven; add water and bring to a boil. Reduce to simmer and cook for 2 hours, covered. Remove from pan, cool, and shred pork. Serves 6.

Overnight Pickin' Pork

Fresh pork shoulder or butt half of fresh ham
Vinegar
Seasoned pepper

Trim skin and brine from ham, leaving a small layer of fat for flavoring. Rub liberal amount of vinegar over ham. Cover completely with seasoned pepper, pressing into sides so most of it will adhere. Wrap tightly in heavy-duty foil. Place in roasting pan and bake at 200° overnight, or at least 10 hours. When unwrapped, the pork will fall off the bone, or shred when pulled with a fork. Serve on buns with coleslaw.

Fastest Amphibious Car

The WaterCar Python has a top speed of 60 mph on water, and can accelerate in 4.5 seconds from 0–60 mph on land.

Fruited Crockpot Roast

1 (3- to 4-pound) Boston butt, or pork tenderloin
1–2 teaspoons Greek seasoning
1 (12-ounce) package dried mix fruit
¾ cup water

Season roast on all sides with Greek seasoning. Place in crockpot with dried fruit on top. Add water; cook on HIGH 5 hours or 8 hours on LOW. Let stand for 15 minutes before removing to slicing board. Serve with fruit and juices over slices. Serves 6.

Editor's Extra: May thicken juices with cornstarch if a thicker gravy is desired.

Pork Chop Dinner in a Dish

6 pork chops
6 medium potatoes, peeled, sliced
1 (4-ounce) can sliced mushrooms, drained
1 (1-ounce) package onion soup mix
1 cup water

Brown pork chops in skillet. Transfer to flat casserole dish. Cover with sliced potatoes, mushrooms, and soup mix; pour water over all. Cover with foil; bake at 350° for 1¼–1½ hours till potatoes are done. Serves 6.

Quick Batter-Fried Pork Chops

4–6 thin-sliced breakfast pork chops
1–2 teaspoons Creole seasoning or seasoned salt
½ cup flour
1 egg mixed with 2 tablespoons milk
1–2 tablespoons vegetable oil

Sprinkle pork chops with seasoning on both sides; pat into meat. Dip each chop into flour, then in egg wash, and back into flour. Place on rack a few minutes for coating to set. Place in skillet with hot oil, and cook on medium-high about 5 minutes per side, till golden brown. Serves 4–6.

Lazy Man's Fried Pork Chops

1 envelope onion soup mix
⅔ cup dry bread crumbs
8 (½-inch-thick) pork chops
2 eggs, well beaten
3 tablespoons butter, melted

Combine soup mix with bread crumbs. Coat chops with egg, then dip in bread crumb mixture, coating well. Place in lightly greased baking pan and drizzle with melted butter. Bake in 325° oven, turning once, till chops are done, about one hour. Serves 8.

Grilled Teriyaki Pork Chops

½ cup teriyaki marinade and sauce
2 tablespoons prepared horseradish
⅛ teaspoon ground cinnamon
4 (¾-inch-thick) pork loin chops

Combine marinade, horseradish, and cinnamon. Marinate pork chops in mixture in large plastic food storage bag. Press air out and seal; turn to coat. Refrigerate 1 hour, turning once. Reserving marinade, remove chops; grill 5–7 inches from medium-hot coals. Cook 10–12 minutes, turning over and brushing with reserved marinade. Serves 4.

Taste of the Islands Pork Chops

6 boneless pork chops
1 (20-ounce) can pineapple slices, drained, reserve juice
⅓ cup honey
2 tablespoons soy sauce
¼ teaspoon ground ginger

Broil pork chops 7 minutes about 5 inches from heat. Turn chops and broil 5 minutes on other side. Combine ¼ cup reserved pineapple juice with honey, soy sauce, and ginger. Put pineapple slices on top of pork chops and broil 6–7 minutes, basting with juice mixture. Spoon remaining juice over chops when serving. Serves 6.

Apricot Pork Loin Chops

1 (8-ounce) jar apricot preserves
¼ cup Italian salad dressing
1½ tablespoons spicy mustard
4 boneless pork loin chops

Combine preserves, dressing, and mustard. Pour ¾ cup mixture into shallow dish; place pork chops in mixture. Refrigerate, covered, to marinate overnight. Refrigerate remaining marinade for basting in a separate container.

Grill drained pork chops over medium heat 4–5 minutes on each side, basting with reserved marinade. Serves 4.

Pork Chops and Apricots

Dee-licious!

6 pork chops
Seasoned flour
1 (16-ounce) can apricot halves, undrained
1 medium onion, finely chopped

Dredge pork chops in seasoned flour; brown in small amount of shortening. Add apricots and onion. Simmer covered till juice thickens, about 20 minutes, then remove cover and simmer another 20–25 minutes. Serves 6.

How fast is a penguin?

The gentoo penguin has a burst speed of about 17 mph.

155

For **faster meal preparation**, do a little planning ahead of time. Have "everything in place." The French term is "mise en place" (MEEZ ahn plahs). Have all your ingredients peeled, cut, chopped, grated, or measured out before starting your recipe.

Cranberry-Onion Chops

4 boneless pork chops
1 (8-ounce) bottle French dressing
1 package onion soup mix
1 (16-ounce) can whole cranberry sauce

Sear pork chops on one side over medium heat in nonstick pan. Stir together remaining ingredients. Turn chops; pour mixture over chops in skillet. Bring to a boil. Lower heat; cover and simmer till chops are just done, about 10 minutes. Serves 4.

Ranch Dressing Pork Chops

1 (1-ounce) package dry ranch dressing mix
4 boneless pork chops

Place dry ranch dressing in gallon zipper bag. Add chops and shake to evenly coat. Refrigerate for 10–15 minutes to allow meat to absorb flavors. Bake in lightly greased baking dish at 350° for 35–45 minutes, depending on thickness of chops. Serves 4.

Smothered Pork Chops

This is sooo good.

6 pork chops
Flour (about ½ cup)
1 (10¾-ounce) can cream of mushroom soup
1 soup can water
1–2 tablespoons Worcestershire

Sprinkle pork chops with salt and pepper to taste; coat with flour. Fry in a little oil till meat is brown. Remove from skillet. Add several teaspoons flour to drippings in skillet; add mushroom soup, water, and Worcestershire. When hot, return pork chops to skillet. Place in 350° oven about 30 minutes. Serves 6.

Grilled Marinated Honey Pork Chops

¼ cup honey
3 tablespoons soy sauce
3 tablespoons lemon juice
1 teaspoon minced garlic
4–5 (1-inch-thick) pork loin chops

Put honey, soy sauce, lemon juice, and garlic in a zipper seal bag; add pork chops and seal. Turn bag over several times to coat chops; refrigerate 3–6 hours or overnight. Drain, discarding marinade. Grill over medium heat, covered, for 12 minutes or more until juices run clear. Serves 4–5.

Inside-Out BBQ Ribs

The secret to these great ribs is the simmer before grilling.

1 (32-ounce) container beef broth
4 racks baby back ribs, quartered
1 (18-ounce) jar barbecue sauce
1 cup honey

In a Dutch oven, bring broth and ribs to a boil, adding water to cover, if necessary. Reduce heat and simmer 1 hour or more till tender.

Place ribs on heated grill; baste generously with a mixture of barbecue sauce and honey. Grill, uncovered, 4 minutes per side. Serves 6.

Juicy Fruited Ribs

These ribs need bibs.

1½ pounds boneless country-style pork ribs
1–2 tablespoons oil
½ cup orange or apricot marmalade
⅓ cup teriyaki sauce
1 teaspoon minced garlic

Brown ribs in oil in skillet. Combine remaining ingredients. Pour half the marmalade mixture in bottom of slow cooker; place ribs on top. Drizzle with remaining marmalade mixture. Cover and cook on LOW 6–8 hours, or till meat is tender. Serves 4.

Tangy Grilled Ham Steak

1 (1½-inch-thick) ham steak
½ cup peach or apricot preserves

Grill ham steak on grill over medium heat 20–25 minutes with closed lid. Turn occasionally till heated through. Spread ham with preserves. Continue to cook over low heat 5–10 minutes or till meat is browned and top is glazed. Serves 4–6.

Ham and Potato Bake

1½–2 cups cooked, cubed ham
6 cups cubed potatoes
1 (10¾-ounce) can cream of celery soup
2 tablespoons butter, melted

Combine all ingredients, add salt and pepper to taste, and bake at 350° in greased casserole dish about 50 minutes, till potatoes are done. Serves 6.

Skillet Ham Slices

1 ham steak, cut ½ inch thick
Brown sugar
Black pepper

Heat lightly greased skillet to medium heat. Rub ham slice on both sides with brown sugar and black pepper. Pan-fry ham about 10 minutes; turn heat off and cover for 5–10 minutes before serving. Cut into serving-size pieces and serve with hot biscuits and jelly or syrup for a delicious supper. Serves 4.

Quickie One-Dish Meal

1 (5.5-ounce) package au gratin potatoes
1 (15-ounce) can mixed vegetables, drained
1 cup cooked, cubed ham, turkey, or chicken
3 tablespoons bread crumbs

Combine potatoes, veggies, and ham in greased casserole. Cover with bread crumbs. Cook according to au gratin package directions. Serves 6.

Crescent Crust Sausage Bake

1 (8-count) can crescent rolls, divided
1 pound ground sausage
2 (10-ounce) cans Ro-Tel tomatoes
2 (8-ounce) packages cream cheese

Line bottom of 8- or 9-inch-square baking pan with ½ the crescent rolls pinched together to fit pan. Brown meat in skillet; add Ro-Tel and cream cheese; stir till smooth; heat through. Pour mixture over bottom crust. Arrange remaining rolls over top, pinching seams for a smooth crust. Bake according to directions on roll package. Serves 4–6.

Fastest Time Around the World by a Sailing Crew

Bruno Peyron (France) with a crew of 14, sailed around the world in 50 days, 16 hours, 20 minutes, and 4 seconds aboard a maxi catamaran in 2005, starting and finishing in Ushant, France.

Cabbage and Weiner Casserole

1 head cabbage, shredded, divided
1 onion, chopped
1 (8-count) package weiners
1 tablespoon brown sugar
1 (10¾-ounce) can tomato soup

Put half the cabbage in bottom of a deep casserole dish that has been sprayed with nonstick spray. Sprinkle onion and salt and pepper over cabbage. Cut weiners into bite-size pieces and put on top of cabbage and onion. Sprinkle with brown sugar. Put other half of cabbage on top of weiners. Pour tomato soup on top. Cover and bake at 350° for 1 hour. Serves 6–8.

State Fair Corn Dogs

2 cups self-rising flour
½ cup cornmeal
1 cup milk
1 package hot dogs
Oil for frying

Combine flour, cornmeal, and milk (batter will be lumpy). Dry hot dogs with paper towel. Cover hot dogs well with batter. Drop in hot vegetable oil in deep-fryer or a pot big enough for hot dogs to float to the top. (If the oil is not hot enough, the mixture will not stay on the hot dog. Test your oil by dropping a little batter in pot; if the oil is hot enough, the batter will float to the top.) Turn the hot dogs as needed to get an even color. Serves 8.

Editor's Extra: Add ¼ cup sugar to batter for sweeter corn dogs.

More **Fast and Fabulous**

FIVE ★ STAR

Poultry

Grilled Lemon Chicken

2 whole chickens, quartered
¾ cup oil
½ cup lemon juice
1 (1.6-ounce) package McCormick Grill Mates Baja Citrus Marinade

Marinate chickens in combined oil, lemon juice, and marinade mix. Cover tightly. Refrigerate for 6 hours, turning chicken occasionally. Remove from refrigerator 1 hour before grilling. Grill 40–45 minutes on medium heat, turning and basting several times. Serves 8–10.

Fabulous Grilled Chicken Halves

¼ cup olive oil
¼ cup Worcestershire
½ cup vinegar
2 teaspoons garlic salt
1 whole chicken, cut in half

Mix first 4 ingredients. Brush chicken on both sides with mixture. Grill 25 minutes on one side, then turn, and grill 25 minutes more. Ten minutes before chicken is done, baste chicken with additional sauce. Serves 2–4.

French Dressing Baked Chicken

1 whole chicken, cut up
1 (8-ounce) bottle French salad dressing
1 package dry onion soup mix

Place chicken in 9x13-inch baking dish. Combine dressing and soup mix; pour over chicken. Bake uncovered at 350° for 1 hour and 20 minutes. Serves 4–6.

Cranberry Chicken

1 (16-ounce) can whole cranberry sauce
1 cup bottled Russian salad dressing with honey
1 package dry onion soup mix
1 (2- to 2½-pound) fryer, cut up

Stir together cranberry sauce, dressing, and soup mix. Place chicken pieces in single layer in baking pan; pour sauce over; cover with foil, and marinate overnight. Without draining, bake at 300° for 2½ hours, uncovered. Serves 6.

Easy Roasted Chicken

1 whole fryer
1 pound carrots, cut in chunks
4 potatoes, unpeeled, quartered
4 onions, peeled, quartered
1 pound fresh mushrooms

Put chicken and vegetables in large roasting pan; salt and pepper to taste; cover with foil. Place in cold oven (it isn't necessary to add water). Turn oven to 250°. Bake 4–5 hours. Serves 4–6.

Easy Oven Chicken

1 chicken, cut into serving pieces
1 envelope mushroom onion soup mix
1 (10¾-ounce) can cream of mushroom soup
1 soup can water

Place chicken in greased 9x13-inch baking dish. Sprinkle with dry soup mix. Mix mushroom soup with water and pour over chicken pieces. Bake, covered, at 350° for 45 minutes, then uncover and continue baking another 15 minutes. Serves 4.

A man followed a **fast** chicken running alongside the road, getting up to 75 mph. When the chicken ran off into a farm, he noticed that it had three legs. He got out of his car and saw that all the chickens running around him had three legs. When he asked the farmer, he replied that everybody at the dinner table fought over the legs, so he bred a three-legged bird. "It's going to make me a millionaire." "How do they taste?" the man asked. "Don't know yet . . . haven't been able to catch one."

Classic Baked Chicken with Gravy

Serve with mango chutney and Spanish rice for a delicious combination.

2–3 tablespoons olive oil
1 (3- to 4-pound) chicken, cut up, rinsed, dried
½ cup chicken broth or white wine (optional)

Lightly coat bottom of roasting pan with olive oil. Rub olive oil over chicken. Sprinkle with salt and pepper. Arrange chicken skin side up in roasting pan, putting breasts in the center. Bake 30 minutes at 400°, then lower heat to 350° and bake about 20 minutes more, or till juices run clear when poked with a sharp knife. Put chicken under broiler for last 5 minutes of cook time to brown.

To make gravy, combine chicken broth or wine and pan drippings (scrape bottom of roasting pan, too) in saucepan and cook on medium till heated through. Serves 4.

Great Bag o' Chicken

1 fryer, cut up
2 tablespoons onion flakes
1 envelope ranch dressing mix

Place chicken in brown-and-serve baking bag. Mix onion flakes, dressing mix, and salt and pepper to taste. Pour over chicken and close bag with twist tie. Place in 350° oven for 1 hour and 15 minutes. Serves 4–6.

Overnight Chicken

1 stick butter, melted
Juice of 2 lemons
1 tablespoon Greek Seasoning
1 fryer, cut up

Mix together butter, lemon juice, and seasoning. Pour over chicken pieces in zipper bag; toss to coat well. Refrigerate overnight. Place chicken in lightly greased baking dish, skin side up, and bake uncovered for 45 minutes at 325°. Serves 4–6.

Truly Southern Fried Chicken

1 fryer, cut up
2 cups buttermilk
1½ cups all-purpose flour
Salt, black pepper, cayenne pepper to taste
2 cups Crisco shortening

Wash chicken and pat dry. Place in large bowl of buttermilk and refrigerate for at least 6 hours. Drain chicken when ready to fry. Mix flour with salt, black pepper, and cayenne to taste. Dredge chicken pieces in mixture, one piece at a time; set aside on wax paper. Heat shortening on medium-high in large, heavy skillet or Dutch oven. Place chicken pieces in hot shortening and fry uncovered about 15 minutes, or till golden brown. Turn chicken and cover lightly (leave room for steam to escape). Fry 15 minutes longer; drain well. Serves 4–6.

Garlic Chicken

20 cloves garlic
6 tablespoons butter
1 chicken, cut up
1 cup chicken broth

Separate garlic into individual cloves; do not peel. Melt butter in skillet. Add chicken and garlic. Sauté, covered, about 20 minutes, turning once. Remove chicken; season to taste. Add chicken broth to skillet and bring to a boil; reduce to ¾ cup. Return chicken; heat. Good over rice. Serves 4–6.

Editor's Extra: Garlic can be removed, but delicious to squeeze out of its skin into your mouth!

Buttermilk Ranch Chicken

⅔ cup dried seasoned bread crumbs
1 (1-ounce) envelope dry buttermilk ranch salad
  dressing mix
½ cup sour cream
4 boneless, skinless chicken breasts, halved
  lengthwise (or 16 chicken tenders)

Preheat oven to 400°. Combine bread crumbs and ranch dressing mix in gallon zipper bag. Place sour cream in shallow dish. Coat chicken breasts with sour cream, then coat with bread crumb mixture. Sprinkle with pepper, if desired. Place in baking pan and bake about 20 minutes. Serves 4.

Honey Mustard Chicken

½ cup honey mustard
¼ cup honey
1 teaspoon Greek seasoning
1 teaspoon Worcestershire
1 (3-pound) fryer chicken, halved, skin on

Combine all but chicken. Spoon some of mixture under loosened skin of chicken. Grill over medium heat on inside halves about 20 minutes. Baste and turn, grill another 20–30 minutes till juices run clear; baste again. Remove skin and cut individual pieces before serving. Serves 2–6.

Crunchy Onion-Crusted Chicken

1½–2 cups French fried onions
1 cup honey mustard
6 boneless, skinless chicken breasts

Crush onions in plastic zipper bag. Spread mustard thickly and evenly on top side of chicken in Pam-sprayed baking pan. Coat with onion crumbs, pressing gently to coat. Bake at 350° for 20 minutes or till chicken is no longer pink. Serves 6.

Tangy Broiled Chicken

½ cup mayonnaise
1 tablespoon honey
2 tablespoons Dijon mustard
4 boneless, skinless chicken breasts

Combine first 3 ingredients. Cover chicken with half the mixture; broil 8–10 minutes. Turn chicken over and spread with remaining mixture. Broil 8–10 minutes more. Serves 4.

The term **"in a jiffy"** dates from the late 1700s. The word jiffy means "a short time."

Fab & more taste

No-Peek Chicken

1 cup white rice (not instant)
2 (10¾-ounce) cans cream of mushroom (or celery) soup
1⅓ cups hot water
4 boneless, skinless chicken breasts
1 envelope dried onion soup mix

Place raw rice in a greased 9x13-inch casserole dish. Combine soup with water and pour over rice. Place chicken on top of soup and sprinkle with soup mix. Cover with foil. Bake at 325° for 2 hours without peeking. Serves 4.

Crunchy Baked Chicken

1⅓ cups cornflake crumbs
1 (1.6-ounce) package zesty herb seasoning mix
6 boneless, skinless chicken breasts
¼ cup buttermilk

Mix crumbs with seasoning mix in plastic zipper bag. Dip chicken in buttermilk. Place in bag with crumb mixture and shake to coat. Bake in greased baking dish at 400° for 45 minutes or till done. Serves 6.

Sweet Jalapeño Chicken

4 chicken breasts, cubed
1 (20-ounce) can pineapple chunks
½ cup sliced jalapeños

Pan-fry chicken till browned; drain grease. Add pineapple with juice. Add jalapeño peppers and juice. Cook over medium-low heat till juices cook off. Serves 4.

Aloha Chicken

2 boneless, skinless chicken breasts, cut bite-size
1 (8-ounce) can pineapple chunks or tidbits, drained
1 (16-ounce) package frozen oriental vegetables
1 (10-ounce) jar sweet and sour sauce

In large nonstick skillet sprayed lightly with cooking spray, brown chicken. Stir in remaining ingredients; simmer, covered, 25 minutes. Serve over rice, if desired. Serves 4–6.

Chicken with Peaches

A delicious and different combination.

2 strips bacon
6 boneless skinless chicken thighs
Celery salt to taste
Onion powder to taste
1 (15-ounce) can peach halves in own juice

Fry bacon in skillet; cool, crumble, and reserve drippings in skillet. Season chicken with celery salt and onion powder. Place in skillet and brown on both sides in bacon drippings. Add peaches and juice; cover and simmer about 45 minutes. Place chicken on platter surrounded by peaches; sprinkle crumbled bacon on peaches. Serves 3–6.

Cheesy Chicken on the Ritz

4 boneless, skinless chicken breasts
½ stick butter, melted
½ cup grated Parmesan cheese
½ cup Ritz Cracker crumbs

Season chicken breasts with salt and pepper to taste. Dip into melted butter. Combine Parmesan and cracker crumbs; coat chicken with mixture. Place in greased baking dish and bake at 350° for about 35 minutes, or till done. Serves 4.

Editor's Extra: This is good using seasoned crouton crumbs.

Ritzy Legs

1 cup crushed Ritz Crackers
3 tablespoons dry vegetable soup mix
1 stick butter, melted
10–12 chicken legs, skin removed

Mix cracker crumbs and soup mix in plastic bag. Dip chicken into melted butter, then coat well with cracker mixture. Place in 9x13-inch baking pan; pour remaining butter over. Bake at 375° for 35–45 minutes, or till done. Serves 8.

Editor's Extra: An envelope of ranch dressing mix subs for the dry soup mix quite tastily.

Stephanie's Easy Italian Chicken

9–10 pieces chicken
1 cup tomato juice
1 teaspoon salt
½ teaspoon oregano
½ teaspoon garlic powder

Roll chicken pieces in tomato juice, and place in large shallow baking dish. Combine remaining ingredients and sprinkle over chicken. Bake at 350° for 50 minutes. Turn and baste with pan juices; bake 40 minutes more. Serves 6–8.

Juicy Chicken Italian

3 pounds boneless, skinless chicken breasts
1 cup Italian salad dressing
1 (14½-ounce) can stewed Italian tomatoes
1½ cups grated mild cheese

Arrange chicken in a 9x13-inch baking dish and pour dressing over, then tomatoes. Bake 20 minutes in 350° oven. Cover with cheese and bake 10–15 minutes, till chicken is done and cheese melted. Serves 6.

Holly's Throw-In-The-Pan Chicken

3 pounds chicken breasts
½ cup Italian dressing

Sprinkle chicken with salt to taste, and brush with dressing. Place chicken in broiler pan on broiler rack 5 inches from heat source. Broil 45 minutes, basting with remaining dressing and turning frequently. Serves 4.

Fastest SMS (Texting)

Melissa Thompson of Salford, UK, broke the record for speed-texting in August 2010. She tapped out the below text in just 25.94 seconds:

The razor-toothed piranhas of the genera Serrasalmus and Pygocentrus are the most ferocious freshwater fish in the world. In reality they seldom attack a human.

(SMS is an acronym for Short Message Service.)

Fastest Computer

Unveiled at the Annual Meeting of National High Performance Computing (HPC China 2010) in Beijing, Tianhe-1A is the world's **fastest** supercomputer with a performance record of 2.507 petaflops. It cost $88 million; its 103 cabinets weigh 155 tons, and the entire system consumes 4.04 megawatts of electricity.

Tianhe-1A ousted the previous record holder, Cray XT5 Jaguar, which is used by the U.S. National Center for Computational Sciences at Oak Ridge National Laboratories. It achieves a performance record of 1.75 petaflops.

Crockpot Chicken and Gravy

1 (0.7-ounce) package dry Italian salad dressing mix
1 (8-ounce) package cream cheese, softened
1 (10¾-ounce) can cream of chicken soup
1 (10¾-ounce) can cream of broccoli soup
4 boneless, skinless chicken breasts

Combine all ingredients in crockpot over chicken. Cook on LOW 6–8 hours. Makes a tasty gravy. Serve over rice, noodles, or mashed potatoes. Serves 4.

Zipper BBQ Chicken

4 boneless, skinless chicken breasts
¼ cup Italian seasoning
1 cup barbecue sauce

Place chicken and seasoning in plastic zipper bag; toss to coat. Remove chicken to a lightly greased 9x13-inch baking dish. Bake at 350° for 20 minutes. Dip chicken in barbecue sauce, then return to oven and bake 20 minutes more; serve with additional barbecue sauce. Serves 4.

Honey BBQ Glazed Kabobs

4 boneless, skinless chicken breast halves, cut into cubes
Vegetables, cut into 1- to 2-inch pieces (onions, mushrooms, bell peppers, squash)
¾ cup honey-flavored barbecue sauce

Thread chicken cubes and vegetables onto skewers, alternating each. Spray with cooking spray. Grill over medium heat 12–15 minutes, turning often, till chicken is cooked. Brush with sauce; grill until kabobs are brown and glazed, about 5 minutes. Makes 4 servings.

Simply Divine Chicken Breast

4 boneless, skinless chicken breasts
4 teaspoons parsley flakes
Garlic salt to taste
¼ cup butter, melted
1 cup herb stuffing mix, crushed

Flatten chicken breast slightly. Sprinkle breasts with parsley and garlic salt; roll up and secure with a toothpick. Roll in butter, then stuffing mix. Place in a well-greased baking dish. Sprinkle remaining crumbs over chicken; drizzle with remaining butter and a little water. Bake at 325° for 30–40 minutes. Serves 4.

Grecian Accent Chicken

Leaving the skin on is the secret to moist, flavorful, and beautiful chicken breasts. This is so easy and yummy.

6 chicken breasts, with skin on
2 tablespoons Greek seasoning
2 Vidalia onions, sliced thickly

Preheat oven to 325°. Sprinkle chicken breasts generously on both sides with Greek seasoning. Place onion slices in bottom of cast-iron Dutch oven and place chicken breasts on top. Cover with lid or foil and bake 1½ hours, till chicken is tender. Serves 6.

Isle of Capri Chicken

8 boneless, skinless chicken breasts
2 tablespoons oil
1 stick butter
2 tablespoons lime juice
2 envelopes Italian salad dressing mix

In skillet, brown chicken breasts in oil. Preheat oven to 325°. In 9x13-inch baking dish, melt butter; add lime juice; stir well. Place chicken in baking dish, turning to coat in mixture. Sprinkle with salad dressing mix. Cover and bake for 1 hour. Serves 6–8.

Monterey Chicken

4 boneless, skinless chicken breasts
1 (8-ounce) block Monterey Jack cheese
2 eggs, beaten
¾ cup dry bread crumbs
2 tablespoons margarine

Flatten each chicken breast to ¼-inch thickness; season with salt and pepper to taste. Cut cheese into 8 sticks. Roll chicken breast around cheese and secure with toothpick. Dip chicken into eggs, then coat with bread crumbs. Brown chicken on all sides in ovenproof skillet in margarine. Remove toothpicks and bake at 400° for 20 minutes. Serves 8.

Queso Chicken on Spanish Rice

1 (12-ounce) box Spanish rice mix
1 (14½-ounce) can chili tomatoes
4 boneless, skinless chicken breasts
1 cup queso dip

Pour rice (with water called for on package) and canned tomatoes into lightly greased baking dish, stirring together. Sear chicken in a lightly oiled skillet until outside is starting to brown. Place chicken over rice and cover with foil. Bake at 350° for 30 minutes; remove foil and pour dip over top. Bake 15 more minutes, or till done. Serves 4.

Maple Grilled Chicken

½ cup maple syrup
½ cup barbecue sauce
½ teaspoon Cajun seasoning
6 boneless, skinless chicken breast halves

Mix syrup, barbecue sauce, and seasoning; reserve ½ cup. Put chicken in remainder of sauce and stir to coat. Grill 6 minutes or longer till juices run clear. Baste with reserved sauce; turn occasionally. Offer remaining sauce at table. Serves 6.

The term **"in a flash"** dates from about 1800. It alludes to a flash of lightning. A bolt of lightning can travel at speeds of 140,000 mph, and can reach temperatures approaching 54,000°F. There are some 16 million lightning storms in the world every year.

Fastest Wind Speed

A wind speed of 253 mph was recorded at Barrow Island, Australia, on April 10, 1996, during Tropical Cyclone Olivia. This is the **fastest** wind speed ever recorded on Earth not associated with a tornado.

Grilled Stuffed Chicken Breasts

4 boneless, skinless chicken breast halves
4 slices thin deli honey ham
4 slices Swiss cheese
1 tablespoon vegetable oil
½ cup seasoned bread crumbs

Pound chicken to flatten to ¼-inch thickness; fit ham and cheese on each; fold in half. Secure with toothpicks. Brush with oil; roll in crumbs. Grill over medium heat approximately 15 minutes, till juices run clear. Serves 4.

Foiled Chicken in Cream Sauce

6 boneless, skinless chicken breasts
Lemon pepper to taste
1 (10¾-ounce) can cream of chicken soup
1 (3-ounce) package cream cheese, softened
1 cup sour cream

Place chicken in greased baking pan; sprinkle with lemon pepper. Mix remaining ingredients and pour over chicken. Cover with foil and bake 2 hours at 300°. Uncover and bake 1 hour longer. Serves 4–6.

Chicken in Butter Cream Sauce

Sauce is great for dipping and sopping!

1½ pounds chicken tenders, breasts, or strips
½ stick butter, divided
1 pint heavy cream

Season chicken tenders with salt and pepper. Sauté chicken in ½ the butter till golden on both sides, about 10 minutes. Add remaining butter, reduce heat to medium, and cook 5 minutes more. Heat cream in skillet; simmer gently, stirring occasionally, until thickened, about 5 minutes, or till chicken is done. Serves 4–6.

Chicken and Asparagus

8 ounces boneless, skinless chicken breasts, cut into strips
10–12 fresh asparagus spears, trimmed
1 (10-ounce) can cream of mushroom soup
½ cup mayonnaise
1 tablespoon lemon juice

Sauté chicken strips for 3 minutes in large skillet sprayed with nonstick cooking spray. Arrange asparagus spears in 8x8-inch baking dish sprayed with nonstick cooking spray. Arrange chicken strips over asparagus; salt and pepper to taste. Combine soup, mayonnaise, and lemon juice with pan drippings in skillet. Cook over low heat 1–2 minutes. Pour soup mixture over chicken. Bake, covered, at 375° for 30 minutes. Uncover and bake 10 minutes longer. Let stand 5 minutes before serving. Serves 4.

Editor's Extra: May sprinkle shredded cheese over soup mixture before baking, if desired.

Lickety Lemon Crispy Chicken

1 pound skinless, boneless chicken tenders
2 tablespoons lemon juice
2 tablespoons butter
½ cup cornflake crumbs

Sprinkle chicken with lemon juice, salt and pepper to taste. Melt butter in a large casserole dish. Place cornflake crumbs on wax paper; roll chicken in crumbs. Place in casserole dish. Bake 15 minutes at 400°; turn and bake another 10 minutes or till chicken is done. Serves 4.

Juicy Sweet and Sour Chicken Tenders

Enough sauce to serve over rice. Delish!

1 (8-ounce) jar orange marmalade
2 tablespoons mayonnaise
1 (8-ounce) bottle Italian dressing
1 envelope onion soup mix
15–20 chicken tenders

Combine first 4 ingredients. Place chicken in bottom of lightly greased baking pan. Pour marmalade mixture over chicken. Bake at 350° for about 35 minutes. Serves 4–6.

French Fried Chicken

2 (3-ounce) cans French fried onions, crushed
2 tablespoons flour
10–12 chicken tenders
1 egg, beaten

Mix onions and flour in gallon zipper bag. Dredge tenders in beaten egg, then coat with onion mixture. Place on lightly greased baking pan. Bake at 400° for 15–20 minutes, or till cooked through. Serves 4–5.

less time

Fast

&

Grilled Chicken Pepper Toss

1 tablespoon oil
1 onion, cut in wedges, separated
1 red bell pepper, sliced
1 yellow bell pepper, sliced
**1 (7-ounce) package cooked grilled chicken
  strips**

Heat oil in wok or skillet; add onion and peppers; stir-fry till beginning to tender. Add chicken strips and toss well with onion and peppers; continue to stir-fry till heated thoroughly. May serve over rice or in warm tortillas, if desired. Serves 4.

Fajita Chicken Enchiladas

1 (10-ounce) can green enchilada sauce
6 (10-inch) flour tortillas
¾ cup sour cream
1 (6-ounce) package grilled fajita chicken strips
2 cups shredded Mexican blend cheese

Pour ⅓ of enchilada sauce in bottom of casserole dish. Tear tortillas and place a layer to cover sauce, then spread sour cream over tortilla layer. Put half the chicken strips on top and half the cheese. Repeat layers with sauce, tortillas, sour cream, chicken strips, and cheese. Then pour remaining ⅓ can of sauce over all. Bake in 350° oven 25–30 minutes. Serves 4–6.

Editor's Extra: May add dollops of chunky salsa on top of sour cream layer, if desired.

**Fastest Half
Marathon**

The record for **fastest** half marathon (13.1 miles) is 58:33 minutes. This record was set by Samuel Wanjiru of Kenya in 2007. Lornah Kiplagat of Kenya holds the **fastest** time for a woman at 66:25 minutes.

Old-Fashioned Chicken and Dumplings

1 fryer, cut into serving pieces
2 cups all-purpose flour
1 teaspoon salt
2 tablespoons butter-flavored shortening
1 cup cold water

Boil chicken in salted water to cover till tender; remove chicken, reserving broth. Bone and cut up chicken. Sift flour and salt together. Make a well in center of flour; put shortening and water in well. Mix with your hands till firm and smooth. Place dough on lightly floured surface. Roll very thin with rolling pin. Cut into strips or squares. Drop, one at a time, into boiling chicken broth. Cook 10–15 minutes. Gently add chicken pieces to dumplings; reduce heat and let simmer 10–15 minutes, covered. Season with salt and pepper to taste. Serves 6.

Editor's Extra: May replace 1 cup broth with 1 cup milk before bringing to a boil and adding dumpling strips.

Chicken 'n Dumplins for Two

1 (18¼-ounce) can chicken vegetable soup
2 frozen buttermilk biscuits (from large bag)

Heat soup in saucepan. Microwave biscuits 2–3 minutes on 70% power till thawed. Tear into pieces and put into soup; cover and continue to simmer another 5–10 minutes. Serves 2.

Editor's Extra: Or bake biscuits per oven directions and tear up into soup.

Quick Chick & Dumplings

6–8 chicken wings
3 cups salted water
1 (10¾-ounce) can cream of chicken soup
½ package frozen dumpling strips, broken

Cook chicken wings in salted water (may use celery salt) until tender. Remove wings; reserve broth. Take meat off bones, or just remove skin, and leave meat intact. Add soup to broth. Put dumplings into slowly boiling broth mixture, and cook till tender, 25–30 minutes. Return wings or meat to dumpling mixture; season to taste. Cook 15 minutes longer. Serves 4–6.

Editor's Extra: If mixture is too thick for your taste, add chicken broth to mixture.

Any Night Chicken and Dressing

1 (8-ounce) package herb-flavored stuffing mix
½ (14½-ounce) can chicken broth (more if needed)
4 chicken quarters
2 teaspoons Greek seasoning

Mix stuffing mix according to package directions, using broth rather than water. Pour into greased 9x13-inch baking dish. Place chicken quarters over top and sprinkle with Greek seasoning. Bake covered 35–40 minutes in 350° oven till chicken runs clear when pierced with fork; uncover and bake till chicken browns slightly. Serves 4–8.

Holly's Heinz 57 Chicken

2–3 pounds chicken pieces
2 tablespoons butter or margarine
½ cup Heinz 57 Sauce
½ cup water

Brown chicken in skillet in butter. Combine Heinz 57 Sauce and water; pour over chicken. Cover; simmer, basting occasionally, 35–40 minutes or until chicken is tender. Remove cover during last 10 minutes of cooking. Spoon sauce over chicken to serve. Serves 4–6.

Crescent Chicken Ring

1 (12-ounce) can chicken
1 (10¾-ounce) can cream of chicken soup
¼ cup chopped onion
1 cup shredded Cheddar cheese
2 (8-count) cans crescent rolls

Drain and flake chicken; mix with soup, onion, cheese, salt and pepper to taste. On lightly greased pizza pan, place crescent rolls, tips to outside of pan. Spoon chicken mixture onto crescent ring. Fold crescent tips back over chicken mixture and tuck under inside ring. Bake at 375° for 15–20 minutes. Serves 6.

Biscuit Chicken Pot Pie

6 boneless, skinless chicken thighs, cooked, diced
1 (10¾-ounce) can cream of chicken soup
1 (14½-ounce) can chicken broth
1 (14-ounce) package frozen mixed vegetables
1 (8-count) can biscuits

Combine all ingredients except biscuits. Place in lightly greased casserole dish; salt and pepper to taste. Place flattened biscuits on top and bake 35–40 minutes at 350°. Serves 6.

Shortcut Chicken

1 (10¾-ounce) can cream of chicken soup
¼ cup milk
3 cups diced cooked chicken
1 small can English peas
1 tablespoon chopped pimentos

In nonstick saucepan, combine soup and milk. Add remaining ingredients; stirring often, bring almost to a boil. Remove from heat. Season with salt and pepper to taste. Serve over biscuits or noodles of choice. Serves 6–8.

Cheddar Cheese Sauce

1 (10¾-ounce) can cream of chicken soup
⅛ teaspoon nutmeg
1 cup grated Cheddar cheese

Heat ingredients over low heat, stirring constantly until cheese is melted. Serve over chicken, vegetables, or rice dishes. Serves 4.

Editor's Extra: Try other cheeses and soups for different flavors.

The term **"snail mail"** was named after the snail with its slow speed. It refers to communication carried by conventional postal delivery services. The phrase refers to the lag-time between dispatch of a letter and its receipt, versus the virtually instantaneous dispatch and delivery of its electronic equivalent, e-mail.

Buffalo Wing Turkey Burgers

1 pound ground turkey
4 teaspoons water
2 tablespoons hickory barbecue seasoning, divided
Buffalo wing seasoning, divided

With hands, combine turkey, water, and ½ the seasoning. Shape into 4 burgers. Season evenly on both sides with remaining seasoning. Grill over medium heat, turning several times, until burgers are browned on both sides and cooked through. Serves 4.

Editor's Extra: You can sub a dash of liquid smoke for the barbecue seasoning in burgers, if you like.

Delicious Doves in Gravy

12 doves
⅓ cup butter or bacon drippings, divided
1 medium onion, chopped
3 tablespoons flour
1½ cups chicken broth

Season doves with salt and pepper. Brown in 4 tablespoons butter or bacon drippings; remove doves. Sauté onion in remaining 2 tablespoons butter; set aside. Stir in flour till light brown. Add chicken broth, stirring constantly for 1 minute; remove from heat; season to taste. Place doves and onion in ovenproof dish and add sauce. Cover and bake at 350° for 1 hour. Serves 6.

less time

Fast

&

More Fast and Fabulous

FIVE ★ STAR

Seafood

World's Fastest Fish

At the top of the list is the Indo-Pacific Sailfish, Istiophorus Platypterus. It has been measured in excess of 68 mph over short periods.

Top Five Fastest Fish

1. Sailfish 68 mph

2. Marlin 50 mph

3. Wahoo 48 mph

4. Tunny 46 mph

5. Bluefish tuna
   44 mph

Silly Salmon Supper

4 (5- to 6-ounce) salmon fillets
½ cup salad dressing (Italian or Caesar)
2 tablespoons soy sauce
1 teaspoon minced garlic

Marinate fillets in zipper bag with salad dressing; refrigerate 2–4 hours. Discard marinade. Grill salmon steaks skin side down on Pam-sprayed rack over medium heat only 5 minutes. Mix soy sauce and garlic; brush over salmon and grill another 12 minutes or so till fish flakes easily with fork. Brush again with sauce before serving. Serves 4.

Broiled Lemon Pepper Salmon

2 tablespoons butter, softened
Zest of 1 lemon
1 teaspoon cracked black pepper
2 salmon fillets

Mix butter, lemon zest, and pepper. Spread over salmon. Broil salmon in oven-proof pan 5–7 inches from heat for 10–15 minutes, till golden. Turn oven off and let sit in oven for 10 more minutes. Serve with lemon wedges. Serves 2.

Baja Salmon

1 package Grill Mates Citrus Baja Marinade
¼ cup oil
2 tablespoons water
2 tablespoons vinegar
2 pounds salmon, other fish, or shrimp

Combine marinade mix with oil, water, and vinegar. Add salmon, coating all sides. Marinate in refrigerator 15 minutes, or longer for extra flavor. Grill, broil, or bake till fish flakes easily with fork, basting with remaining marinade halfway through cooking. Discard any leftover marinade. Serves 4–6.

Honey-Mustard Salmon on Pesto Fettuccine

4 salmon steaks
1 tablespoon butter, melted
1 tablespoon honey mustard
1 (8-ounce) package fettuccine
½ cup pesto

Place salmon steaks in lightly sprayed baking pan; brush with butter and mustard. Bake at 450° for 10 minutes till flaky.

Cook pasta; drain. Toss with pesto and place on serving platter. Place salmon steaks on top. Serve with lemon wedges and parsley, if desired. Serves 4.

Lemon-Dill Salmon Steaks

Microwave easy.

4 salmon steaks
2 tablespoons butter
2 tablespoons fresh lemon juice
¼ teaspoon dill weed

Microwave salmon in paper-towel-lined dish 3–4 minutes, or till flakes easily. Remove to serving plate. Melt butter with lemon juice and dill. Pour over salmon. Garnish with lemon slices, if desired. Serves 4.

Salmon Cups

1 (16-ounce) can salmon, drained, flaked
½ cup seasoned bread crumbs
1 tablespoon butter, melted
2 eggs, beaten
1 tablespoon lemon juice

Combine all ingredients with salt and pepper to taste; mix well. Spoon mixture into 6 oiled muffin cups. Bake at 350° for 30 minutes.

Editor's Extra: May serve with a cheese sauce, if desired.

Snapper in a Packet

4 snapper fillets
Fresh lemon juice
4 thick onion slices
1 green bell pepper, cut in chunks
2 tablespoons butter

Place each fillet on a piece of heavy-duty foil. Season with salt, pepper, and lemon juice to taste. Top with divided onion slices, green pepper, and butter; seal foil, leaving room for expansion. Place on baking sheet; bake at 375° for 25 minutes. Serves 4.

Ranch Baked Fish

This is great with most any flavor of chips.

4 (½-pound) catfish or tilapia fillets
1 cup chopped onion
1 (8-ounce) bottle ranch dressing
2 cups crushed potato chips

Lay fillets in buttered 9x13-inch baking dish; sprinkle with onion. Spread dressing over to completely coat fillets. Sprinkle with crushed potato chips, covering completely. Bake at 350° for 35 minutes. Serves 4.

Flounder with Sour Cream

1 (4-pound) flounder
Butter
Greek seasoning
1½ cups sour cream
¼ cup sliced almonds

Flatten flounder and rub inside and out with butter and seasoning. Place in baking dish. Cover with sour cream; sprinkle with almonds. Cover with foil, and bake at 350° about 45 minutes, or till done. Garnish with fresh parsley or dill. Serves 4–6.

Almond-Crusted Flounder

1 flounder fillet
2 tablespoons butter
¼ cup yogurt
¼ cup sliced almonds, toasted

Rinse and dry fish with paper towels. Season to taste. Sauté in butter till golden, about 5 minutes per side. Turn; paint with yogurt and sprinkle with almonds while other side browns. Transfer to plate and drizzle with remaining butter in pan. Garnish with lemon wedge, if desired. Serves 1.

Editor's Extra: May sprinkle fish fillets with a little Greek seasoning, if desired.

Outstanding Baked Seafood Trio

This has become a favorite in my house. —Barbara Moseley

2 frozen flounder or tilapia fillets, thawed
4 frozen sea scallops, thawed, halved
2 frozen crab cakes, thawed
Juice of 1 lemon
½ stick butter, melted

Pat fillets dry and place in lightly greased baking dish. Top fillets with scallops, then crumble crab cakes over top. Mix lemon juice with melted butter; baste seafood. Place in preheated 400° oven, and bake 20–25 minutes, or till fish flakes easily. Remove to plate and pour pan juices over all. Serves 2.

Fastest Shark

If there was a swimming race, the Shortfin Mako shark would win. According to the ReefQuest Centre for Shark Research, "It has been reliably clocked at 31 mph, and there is a claim that one individual of this species achieved a burst speed of 46 mph."

The record for the **fastest** time for circling the bases on a regulation baseball diamond is 13.3 seconds, set by Evar Swanson at Columbus, Ohio, in 1932. His average speed around the bases was 18.45 mph.

Bacon Seafood Kabobs

1 pound flounder fillets
1 pound bay scallops
8 slices bacon
Fresh lemon juice
Creole seasoning

Cut flounder fillets into 1½-inch pieces. Thread flounder pieces, scallops, and bacon onto 8 skewers, making sure bacon intertwines with each piece of seafood. Sprinkle with fresh lemon juice and Creole seasoning to taste. Broil on rack on baking pan under medium heat till bacon is done, turning to cook on all sides. Serves 6.

Island Fillets

4 fat fish fillets (tilapia or orange roughy)
1 cup sweet and sour sauce

Marinate fish in sweet-and-sour sauce at least 1 hour. Then salt and pepper to taste, and broil on broiler pan 4 inches from heat 3–6 minutes per side. Garnish with orange slices, if desired. Serves 4.

Parmesan Baked Fish Fillets

4 fillets of fish (cod, tilapia, flounder, catfish)
½ cup mayonnaise
¼ cup grated Parmesan cheese
1 teaspoon Worcestershire
¼ cup chopped green onions

Spray baking dish with cooking spray; place fish fillets in dish. Combine remaining ingredients and spread over fillets. Bake, uncovered, 15–20 minutes at 400°, or till fish flakes easily with fork. Serves 4.

I-Yi-Yi Baked Fish

1 pound fish fillets (tilapia, catfish, or orange roughy)
1 (10-ounce) can Ro-Tel tomatoes, well drained
1 (20-ounce) can crushed pineapple, lightly drained
1 tablespoon lemon juice

Wash and paper-towel dry fish fillets; put in large casserole dish; sprinkle with salt and pepper to taste. Mix tomatoes, pineapple, and lemon juice in saucepan and spoon onto fillets. Bake at 400° for 40–50 minutes till fish is flaky. Serve over rice. Serves 4.

Tilapia Fillets on a Bed of Smothered Onions

Even better than it sounds . . . and so quick to fix!

4 tilapia fillets
1 teaspoon Greek seasoning
1 medium onion, sliced
½ stick butter, divided
2 tablespoons lemon juice

Rinse fillets and pat dry with paper towels. Season and set aside. Sauté onion in half of butter till limp on medium-high heat. Remove onions to a plate; add remaining butter to skillet and cook fillets 2 minutes. Turn fillets over, then transfer the onions to the top of the fillets. Now squeeze lemon juice over and cook another 1–2 minutes till lightly browned. Add more seasoning, if desired. Offer tartar sauce. Serves 4.

Cornflake Crusted Tilapia Fillets

Quick from start to finish, and so delicious, nobody will ask for tartar sauce.

1 cup crushed cornflakes
1 teaspoon Mrs. Dash Onion and Herb Seasoning
2 tablespoons Egg Beaters (or one egg white, beaten)
4 thin frozen tilapia fillets
Spray butter

Mix crumbs with seasoning in shallow dish. Pour Egg Beaters in another shallow dish. Dip thawed fillets in egg, then crumbs, coating thickly. Place on foil sprayed with butter spray, then spray crusted fillets with spray butter. Bake 7–8 minutes in 450° oven till flaky. Serves 2–4.

Editor's Extra: I recommend you crush cornflakes in a food processor. Better crush enough for another making . . . it's so good, you'll want to make it again and again.

Surprise Flavored Fish

½ cup pineapple mustard (or other flavor)
½ cup mayonnaise
1½ pounds orange roughy or tilapia

Mix mustard and mayonnaise. Place fish in a shallow oil-sprayed pan. Cover fish completely with mixture. Bake at 350° for 10–15 minutes, just till fish is done. Broil a minute to brown. Serves 4.

Editor's Extra: Pineapple horseradish is delicious as well.

Baked Orange Roughy

2 pounds orange roughy
4 ounces shredded Parmesan cheese
½ cup finely chopped onion
1 cup mayonnaise
1 tablespoon lemon juice

Place fish in buttered dish; cook in preheated 450° oven 10 minutes. If liquid appears, pour off. Mix remaining ingredients and spread over fish. Bake 20–25 minutes till light brown and puffy. Serves 4.

Lemon-Tomato Fish Fillets

1 pound fresh white fish fillets
1 lemon, thinly sliced
1 tomato, thinly sliced
¼ teaspoon thyme
2 tablespoons white wine

Place fillets in single layer in lightly sprayed baking dish. Bake at 500° for 3–5 minutes, or till fillets begin to turn white. Place lemon and tomato slices on fish; sprinkle with thyme and wine. Bake 3–5 minutes longer, or until fish flakes easily. Serves 2.

Crunchy Baked Fish

1 cup soup cream
1 cup mayonnaise
1 envelope ranch-style salad dressing mix
4 pounds fish fillets
1 (3-ounce) can French-fried onions, crushed

Mix sour cream, mayonnaise, and dressing mix. Dip fillets in mixture, then coat with crushed onions. Bake in 350° oven for 14–20 minutes, or until fish flakes easily. Serves 8.

Fastest Swimmer

Breaking 37 world records, Michael Phelps (born June 30, 1985) is generally considered the greatest swimmer of all time. The American swimmer has won 16 Olympic medals—six gold and two bronze at Athens in 2004, and eight gold at Beijing in 2008. In Beijing, all victories but one were accompanied by a world record.

Slow down and enjoy life. It's not only the scenery you miss by going too **fast**—you also miss the sense of where you are going and why.

—*Eddie Cantor*

Creole Catfish Amandine

⅓ cup butter, melted
3 tablespoons lemon juice
4 catfish fillets
1½ teaspoons Creole seasoning
½ cup sliced almonds

Combine butter and lemon juice. Dip fillets in butter mixture. Place in a 9x13-inch baking dish. Sprinkle fish with Creole seasoning and almonds. Bake at 375° for 25–30 minutes or till fish flakes when tested with fork. Serves 4.

Oven-Fried Catfish Nuggets

½ cup seasoned bread crumbs
½ cup crushed cornflakes
¼ cup grated Parmesan cheese
1½ pounds catfish nuggets

Combine bread crumbs, cornflakes, and Parmesan cheese in shallow dish; season to taste. Spray catfish nuggets with butter-flavored cooking spray and dredge in crumb mixture. Bake on sprayed cookie sheet at 375° for 15–20 minutes or till fish flakes easily. Serves 4.

Zippy Fried Catfish

2 pounds catfish fillets
1 cup prepared mustard
3 cups cornmeal or fish fry
2 teaspoons Old Bay Seasoning
3 cups oil for frying

Clean and rinse fillets; pat dry. Coat well with mustard; roll in seasoned cornmeal. Fry in ½ inch or more of hot oil until golden brown; drain on paper towels. Serves 4–6.

Grilled Marinated Shrimp Kabobs

3 pounds peeled, deveined shrimp
8 ounces mushrooms, halved
1 red bell pepper, cut in 1-inch pieces
1 onion, cut in 1-inch pieces
2 cups prepared citrus marinade

Skewer shrimp and vegetables. Cover with marinade, reserving 2 tablespoons for basting. Cover and refrigerate 1 hour. Grill 3–4 minutes on each side over hot coals, basting before turning once. Serves 8.

Cajun Peppered Shrimp

Be brave! This is superb!

2 pounds large headless shrimp, unpeeled
¼ cup ground black pepper (Yes! ¼ cup)
2 sticks butter

Place shrimp in large baking dish; cover with black pepper, then with slices of butter. Cover with foil. Bake at 400° for 10 minutes, then turn shrimp with spatula. Cook another 5–10 minutes, till shrimp turn pink. Pour juices over shrimp when serving. Serves 4–6.

Easy Shrimp Scampi

2 teaspoons olive oil
2 pounds uncooked shrimp, peeled, deveined
¾ cup prepared herb & garlic marinade
¼ cup finely chopped green onions

Heat oil in large skillet over medium heat. Add shrimp and marinade, and cook till shrimp turn pink, 4–5 minutes, stirring constantly. Stir in green onions. Serves 4.

195

Shrimp Stir-Fry

1 (16-ounce) package frozen Chinese vegetables
1 tablespoon soy sauce
1 pound shrimp, peeled, deveined
1 (8-ounce) can chunk pineapple, partially
    drained
2 cups cooked rice

In large skillet or wok, sauté vegetables in soy sauce. Add shrimp and pineapple; simmer, stirring occasionally till shrimp are pink, about 5 minutes. Serve over cooked rice. Pass sweet and sour sauce, if desired. Serves 2–4.

Broiled Chili Shrimp

1 pound large shrimp, peeled, deveined
1 cup prepared chili sauce
14–16 slices bacon, halved

Marinate raw shrimp in chili sauce overnight. Remove shrimp from marinade. Wrap ½ piece bacon around each shrimp; secure with toothpick. Broil shrimp 6 inches from heat for 3–4 minutes till bacon is browned. Turn to brown other side. Serve hot. Serves 6.

Soppin' Shrimp Bake

2 pounds shrimp, unpeeled
2 sticks butter, melted
2 sticks margarine, melted
¼ cup Worcestershire

Place shrimp in 9x13-inch baking pan. Combine butter, margarine, and Worcestershire; pour over shrimp. Bake uncovered at 350° for 30 minutes. Serve with French bread for sopping. Serves 6–8.

Spicy Shrimp Casserole

1 (1-pound) block Velveeta White Queso cheese
2 (10-ounce) cans diced Ro-Tel tomatoes, any
 flavor, drained
2 pounds fresh medium shrimp, cooked, peeled,
 deveined
1 (1-pound) bag long-grain rice, cooked

Melt cheese in Dutch oven over low heat; add Ro-Tel tomatoes.   Heat, then add shrimp and cooked rice; mix well. Spoon into a greased 9x13-inch casserole. Bake 20 minutes at 350°. Serves 8–12.

Battered-Up Shrimp

1½ cups all-purpose flour, divided
½ teaspoon cayenne pepper
1 teaspoon salt
1½ cups flat beer
2 pounds uncooked shrimp, peeled, leaving tails

Mix 1 cup flour, cayenne, and salt in mixing bowl. Slowly add beer until batter is quite thin. Dip shrimp first in remaining ½ cup flour, then into beer batter. Deep-fry in 400° oil for 2 minutes. Drain on paper towels. Serve immediately. Serves 4–6.

Spicy Beer Batter

1 (12-ounce) can beer
1 teaspoon Creole seasoning
2 cups all-purpose flour
1 teaspoon paprika
¾ teaspoon cayenne pepper

Mix all ingredients well. Dip seafood (shrimp, crab claws, or catfish) in batter and deep-fry till golden brown.

Fastest Pumpkin Carving

The **fastest** time to carve a face into a pumpkin (eyes, nose, mouth, ears) is 24.03 seconds, by Stephen Clarke (USA).

Speedo is currently the world's largest-selling swimwear brand, and manufactures products for both recreational and competitive swimming. Formerly McRae Hosiery Manufacturers, the name Speedo was first adopted in 1928 after the firm developed its racerback design of swimwear. The name was made up by a Captain Jim Parsons who won a company competition with the slogan "Speed on in your Speedos."

Crab Cakes the Easy Way

¼ cup finely chopped onion
3 teaspoons vegetable oil, divided
1 pound lump crabmeat
1 egg, beaten
½–¾ cup seasoned bread crumbs

Sauté onion in 1 teaspoon oil till tender. In a bowl, combine crabmeat, egg, and sautéed onion. Shape into 6–8 crab cakes; roll in crumbs. Fry on medium heat in remaining 2 teaspoons oil till golden brown on both sides, about 5 minutes. Drain on paper towels. Serves 3–4.

Pan-Fried Soft-Shell Crabs

2 eggs, beaten
¼ cup milk
2 teaspoons salt, divided
12 soft-shell crabs, rinsed, dried
¾ cup all-purpose flour

Combine eggs, milk, and 1 teaspoon salt. Dip crabs into egg mixture. Combine flour with remaining 1 teaspoon salt. Coat crabs with flour mixture. Pan-fry crabs in hot shortening for 8–10 minutes, turning often. Serves 6.

Rice and Crab Casserole

1 pound bacon, cooked, drained
1 pound crabmeat, lump or claw
3 cups cooked rice
1 cup diced onion

Crumble bacon and mix with crabmeat, rice, and onion; salt and pepper to taste. Pour in lightly greased casserole dish. Bake 25–30 minutes at 350°. Serves 6–8.

Crabmeat Soufflé

1 pound crabmeat
1 cup grated sharp Cheddar cheese
4 eggs, separated
4 tablespoons mayonnaise

Mix crabmeat, cheese, egg yolks, and mayonnaise. Fold in beaten-stiff egg whites. Put in buttered baking dish; cook 20–30 minutes at 375°. Serves 4.

Caley's Crabmeat Sauce

Tastes great on grilled fish, toast, or pasta.

2 tablespoons butter
1 (6- to 7-ounce) package frozen crabmeat, drained
3–4 teaspoons flour
1 cup half-and-half

Heat butter in saucepan; add crabmeat, flour, and a little salt. Blend, then gradually add half-and-half. Cook on medium heat, stirring till thick. Serves 4.

Scallops on Skewers

3 limes
2 pounds sea scallops
6 tablespoons butter, melted
¼ cup grated Parmesan cheese
18 slices Canadian bacon

Halve 1 lime and slice the remaining limes into 18 slices. Drizzle scallops with juice squeezed from lime half. Dip scallops into melted butter; sprinkle with Parmesan cheese. Alternate scallops, lime slices, and folded bacon slices on skewers, and place on hot grill, 4 inches from heat, about 6 minutes. Turn and brush with remaining butter and cheese; broil 6 minutes longer. Serves 4.

Classic Scalloped Oysters

1 cup crushed saltines, divided
1 quart raw oysters, drained
2 eggs
1¾ cups milk
1 stick butter

In buttered baking dish, layer ⅓ of cracker crumbs, then ⅓ of oysters. Repeat layers, reserving ⅓ of crumbs for top. Beat eggs with milk, and pour over top. Sprinkle with remaining crumbs; dot butter over top. Bake at 350° for 20–30 minutes. Serves 6.

Deep-Fried Oysters

1 cup all-purpose flour
2 pints raw oysters
3 eggs, well beaten
1 cup bread crumbs

Mix flour with salt and pepper to taste. Dip oysters in flour mixture, then in beaten eggs, then dip in bread crumbs. Deep-fry in hot oil 2–3 minutes. Drain on paper towels. Serves 4.

Editor's Extra: A great way to serve these delights is in a hoagie bun with lots of oyster cocktail sauce.

Cucumber Sauce for Seafood

Great with any fish, including shellfish.

1 whole cucumber, grated
½ cup sour cream
½ cup plain yogurt
1 tablespoon dried dill
Juice of ½ lemon

Squeeze grated cucumber in paper towels to remove excess water. Combine with remaining ingredients; refrigerate an hour or more to blend flavors.

More **Fast and Fabulous**

FIVE ★ STAR

Cakes

Orange Jell-O Cake

1 (18¼-ounce) box butter cake mix
1 (4-serving) package orange Jell-O
½ teaspoon orange extract
Powdered sugar (optional)

Grease and flour Bundt pan. Prepare cake mix according to package directions. Set 1½ cups batter aside for later; pour remaining batter into pan. Stir dry Jell-O and extract into reserved batter. Drop by tablespoons onto batter in pan. Swirl knife through batter for marbled effect. Bake in 350° oven about 45 minutes or till toothpick inserted in center comes out clean. Allow to cool in pan for 10 minutes, then remove and allow to cool completely. Dust with powdered sugar, if desired. Serves 12–15.

Touch of Orange Cake

1 (18¼-ounce) box yellow cake mix
1 (11-ounce) can Mandarin oranges, undrained
4 eggs
¼ cup oil

Beat all ingredients 2 minutes. Beat on low speed 1 minute longer. Pour batter into greased and floured 9x13-inch pan. Bake at 350° for 30 minutes. Cool. May top with Cool Whip mixed with a few spoonfuls of crushed pineapple, if desired. Serves 12–15.

None-Better Cherry Delight

An easy classic that everybody loves.

1 (21-ounce) can cherry pie filling
1 (6½-ounce) box Jiffy white cake mix
1 stick butter, melted
½ cup chopped pecans or almonds
½ cup flaked coconut

Pour pie filling evenly into a greased square baking pan. Sprinkle dry cake mix over it. Pour melted butter over cake mix; sprinkle with nuts and coconut. Bake at 350° for 55 minutes. Good with ice cream or Cool Whip. Serves 6–9.

Sensational Cherry Dump Cake

2 (16-ounce) cans pitted sour cherries, drained
¾ cup sugar
1 (18¼-ounce) box lemon cake mix
1 stick butter, melted
1 cup chopped pecans (optional)

Pour cherries into 9x13-inch cake pan; sprinkle with sugar. Sprinkle dry cake mix over cherries. Pour melted butter over all. Add nuts last, if desired. Bake in 350° oven 1 hour. Serves 12–15.

Fast Folk Phrases

He cut and ran.

He bailed.

He scooted right out of there.

He was splittin' the mud.

He took off like a scalded dog.

He high-tailed it. (He ran like a wild turkey.)

He slipped out like a greased pig.

He went off like a bat out of hell.

He ran screaming for the hills.

He hit the ground running.

He slipped the noose.

He took off like greased lightning.

Apple-y Spice Cake

1 (18¼-ounce) box spice cake mix
1 large apple, peeled, cored, minced
1 (14-ounce) can sweetened condensed milk
1 cup sour cream
¼ cup lemon juice

Grease and flour 9x13-inch baking pan. Prepare cake mix per package directions; stir in apple; pour into pan. Bake in 350° oven 30–35 minutes until toothpick comes out clean. Combine sweetened condensed milk and sour cream; stir in lemon juice; spread over hot cake. Bake 5 more minutes; sprinkle scantily with cinnamon, if desired. Cool; store covered in refrigerator. Serves 12–15.

Editor's Extra: May sprinkle cake with cinnamon before the last 5 minutes of baking.

Apple-Pineapple Dump Cake

1 (20-ounce) can crushed pineapple, drained
1 (21-ounce) can apple pie filling
1 (18¼-ounce) box yellow or lemon pudding cake mix
1 cup chopped pecans
2 sticks butter, melted

Spread pineapple in bottom of greased 9x13-inch pan. Top with apple pie filling; sprinkle with dry cake mix. Sprinkle nuts over top and pour melted butter over all. Bake at 350° for 40–45 minutes. Serves 12–15.

Pineapple Upside-Down Cake

1 (15-ounce) can pineapple slices
½ cup butter, melted
1 (16-ounce) package brown sugar
1 (8-ounce) can crushed pineapple, drained
1 (18¼-ounce) box butter cake mix

Drain pineapple slices and reserve juice. Mix butter and brown sugar, and pour into a 9x13-inch pan. Arrange pineapple slices over top, then cover with crushed pineapple. Prepare cake mix as package directs, using ⅔ cup reserved pineapple juice for water. Pour batter over pineapple. Bake at 350° for about 50 minutes, or till toothpick inserted in center comes out clean. Invert pan to remove cake, and serve while still warm. Serves 12–15.

Editor's Extra: Pretty to add maraschino cherries to center of pineapple slices, and a dollop of whipped cream on top.

Light and Bright Pineapple Cake

A crowd pleaser!

1 (18¼-ounce) box butter cake mix
1 (20-ounce) can crushed pineapple
1 cup sugar
1 large box vanilla instant pudding
1 (16-ounce) container whipped topping

Preheat oven to 350°. Prepare cake mix according to directions on box, and bake in greased and floured 9x13-inch baking pan for time suggested. Heat pineapple (with juice) and sugar in medium saucepan for about 5 minutes. While cake is still hot, pour hot pineapple mixture over top. Allow to cool. Mix pudding and whipped topping and spread over top of cake. Serves 12–15.

Lemony Lemon Ice Box Cake

**1 (18¼-ounce) box lemon cake mix, prepared
  as directed on box**
1 (14-ounce) can sweetened condensed milk
⅓ cup lemon juice

While cake is still warm, poke small holes in cake (I used a wooden kabob skewer). Mix sweetened condensed milk with lemon juice and pour over cake; cover and refrigerate. Frost with Lemon Cream Cheese Frosting when cake has completely cooled. Keep refrigerated until ready to serve. Serves 12–15.

LEMON CREAM CHEESE FROSTING:

1 (8-ounce) package cream cheese, softened
1 (15-ounce) can lemon cake frosting

Mix cream cheese and lemon frosting until smooth and creamy.

Editor's Extra: To make it even more lemony, add a tablespoon of lemon juice to the frosting.

Strawberry Bundt Cake

An easy classic that never fails to please.

1 (18¼-ounce) box strawberry cake mix
1 (3-ounce) package vanilla instant pudding
4 eggs
1 cup water
½ cup oil

Preheat oven to 350°. Mix ingredients by hand until well combined. Grease a Bundt pan, and pour in batter. Bake for 35–40 minutes, or until done. May glaze with powdered sugar mixed with a little water, if desired. Serves 12–15.

Moist & Delicious Rhubarb Cake

1 (18¼-ounce) box butter cake mix
1½ cups sugar
3 cups finely chopped rhubarb
½ cup whipping cream

Preheat oven to 350°. Grease and flour a 9x13-inch baking dish. Prepare cake according to directions on box. Pour batter into baking dish. Mix sugar with rhubarb, and spread evenly over batter. Pour cream (unwhipped) over top. Bake for 40–45 minutes, or till done. Allow to cool, then serve with sweetened whipped cream, if desired. Serves 12–15.

Upside-Down Rhubarb Cake

A very sweet cake.

4 cups finely chopped rhubarb
1 (3-ounce) package strawberry gelatin
1 cup sugar
3 cups mini marshmallows
1 (18¼-ounce) box butter cake mix

Preheat oven to 350°. Mix rhubarb with gelatin and sugar, and spread evenly over bottom of greased 9x13-inch baking dish. Sprinkle with marshmallows. Prepare cake mix according to package directions and bake 30–35 minutes, or until done. Allow to cool, then flip over. Makes its own topping, but may be served with Cool Whip, if desired. Serves 12–15.

Fastest Ground Vehicle on Wheels

No other ground vehicle can out-accelerate a top-fuel dragster. Drag racers compete to be the first to cross a set finish line, usually from a standing start on a quarter-mile track in a straight line. The **faster** vehicles need a parachute (mandated by rules) to slow down.

Tony Schumacher (Germany) holds the quarter-mile record at 336.15 mph, set in 2009.

Creamy Cranberry Cake

Makes its own yummy sauce.

2 cups self-rising flour
2 cups sugar, divided
½ cup plus 3 tablespoons butter, divided
2 cups heavy cream, divided
1½ cups cranberries

Preheat oven to 350°. Combine flour, 1 cup sugar, 3 tablespoons butter (melted), and 1 cup cream. Stir in cranberries. Bake in greased 9x13-inch pan for 25 minutes, or until done.

Bring remaining 1 cup sugar, ½ cup butter, and 1 cup cream to a boil over medium heat. Boil for 3 minutes, then pour over cooled cake. Serves 12–15.

Editor's Extra: May sub half-and-half for part or all of heavy cream.

Blueberry Coffee Cake

1 (18¼-ounce) box lemon cake mix with pudding
1 stick margarine, softened
⅔ cup milk
2 eggs
1¼ cups blueberries

Combine cake mix and margarine in mixer bowl; mix at low speed until crumbly. Reserve 1¼ cups crumbs for topping. Combine remaining crumbs, milk, and eggs; beat 2 minutes on HIGH. Pour into greased and floured 9x13-inch baking pan. Arrange blueberries evenly over batter; sprinkle with reserved crumbs. Bake at 350° for 35–45 minutes, or until toothpick comes out clean; cool. Serves 12–15.

Yummy Butter Cake

1 (18¼-ounce) box yellow cake mix
4 eggs, divided
1 stick butter, melted
1 (8-ounce) package cream cheese, softened
1 (1-pound) box powdered sugar

Combine cake mix with 2 eggs and butter; spread in bottom of greased 9x13-inch pan. Mix cream cheese with remaining 2 eggs and powdered sugar. Pour over cake mixture. Bake at 350° for 35–40 minutes—no more. Serves 12–15.

Pumpkin Spice Cake

This is so delicious! The creamy frosting is just the topping to lighten up the tasty pumpkin spice cake. —Melinda Burnham

1 cup pumpkin purée from (15-ounce) can
3 large eggs
1 cup water
¼ cup amaretto (optional)

Mix all. Pour into 2 or 3 greased round cake pans or a greased 9x13-inch sheet cake pan. Bake at 325° for 20–25 minutes, a little less time if you divide the batter into 3 cake pans. Allow to cool and frost top, middle, and sides with White Chocolate Mousse Icing. (See below.) Serves 8 or more.

White Chocolate Mousse Icing

3 cups heavy whipping cream, very cold
2 (3-ounce) packages white chocolate instant pudding

In a medium bowl, on high speed, mix until very stiff peaks form. Cover and refrigerate until ready to frost cake. Refrigerate cake after frosting.

All-Fall-Down Pecan Cake

Seems like too little liquid—not. Just do it.

2 cups biscuit mix
2½ cups brown sugar
4 large eggs
1 cup chopped pecans

Mix all well. Bake in greased 9x13-inch pan 40 minutes at 325°. Cake rises, then falls. Serves 12–15.

Editor's Extra: Add a teaspoon of vanilla for a change, but deliciously pecan-y with or without.

Heavenly Delight

2 cups mini marshmallows
6 (1.45-ounce) chocolate bars, chopped
⅔ cup milk
1 (12-ounce) carton Cool Whip, divided
1 angel food cake, prepared

Melt marshmallows and chocolate bars in milk in saucepan. Pour into bowl and cool. Fold in ¾ cup Cool Whip. Cut cake horizontally into 3 layers. Spread ⅓ filling over bottom layer; place second layer and spread ⅓ filling; repeat with top layer and filling. Frost cake with remaining Cool Whip. May add chocolate curls, if desired. Serves 12–15.

Angel Cherry Chip Cake

1 (18¼-ounce) box angel food cake mix
2 egg whites
1 teaspoon almond extract
1 (4½-ounce) jar maraschino cherries, chopped, drained, reserve liquid
1 cup mini chocolate chips

Make angel food cake per package directions using 2 egg whites, almond extract, and the liquid from cherries as part of water called for; beat well. Fold in cherries and chocolate chips. Bake in greased and floured tube pan at 350° for 40–45 minutes. Serves 12–15.

Fastest Ice Climber

Pacel Gulyaev (Russia) climbed a 49-foot high vertical ice wall in 8.748 seconds in Romania on February 8, 2009.

Two-Step Chocolate Cherry Cake

So moist, delicious, and quick, you will make this again and again.

1 (18¼-ounce) dark chocolate cake mix
1 (21-ounce) can cherry pie filling
2 eggs
¼ cup oil
1 teaspoon almond extract

Mix all together by hand. Bake in lightly greased 9x13-inch pan at 375° till middle springs back, 27–35 minutes. Serves 12–15.

Editor's Extra: You can throw in a cup of chocolate (or white) chips if you really want it gooey-er. Or throw them on top of the hot cake when it comes out of the oven. Or sprinkle with powdered sugar. Or, my favorite, serve slices with a generous dollop of whipped cream. But this cake is good all by itself—*really* good.

Double-Decker Delight

1 (18¼-ounce) box German chocolate cake mix
4 eggs, divided use
1 stick butter, softened
1 (8-ounce) package cream cheese, softened
1 (1-pound) package powdered sugar

Combine cake mix, 2 eggs, and butter; mix well. Spread in bottom of greased and floured 9x13-inch baking pan. Mix cream cheese, sugar, and remaining 2 eggs and spread over first layer. Bake at 375° for 45–50 minutes. May sprinkle with chopped nuts before baking, if desired. Serves 12–15.

Chocolate Swirl Cake

The taste and texture are divine.

3 (8-ounce) packages cream cheese, softened
1 cup sugar
5 eggs
1 tablespoon vanilla
1 (4-ounce) package German's sweet chocolate

Beat cream cheese with sugar well. Add eggs, one at a time; add vanilla. Set aside 2 cups mixture in another bowl. Melt chocolate 2 minutes in microwave; stir and cool slightly. Add to 2 cups of set-aside mixture. Pour remaining mixture into greased 9-inch-square pan. Drop chocolate dollops onto white mixture and run knife back and forth through it to marbleize—don't overdo. Bake at 350° for 45 minutes. Cool; then chill. Makes 9 squares.

Caramel Chocolate Gooey Cake

1 (18¼-ounce) box German chocolate cake mix
1 (14-ounce) can sweetened condensed milk
1 (8-ounce) jar caramel topping
1 (8-ounce) carton Cool Whip

Bake cake in a greased 9x13-inch pan according to package directions. While warm, poke holes all over with end of wooden spoon. Pour sweetened condensed milk in holes; pour caramel over cake and refrigerate. Top with Cool Whip to serve. May sprinkle with crushed Heath bars. Serves 12–15.

Chocolate Caramel Cake

Deliciousness—all the way through.

1 (18¼-ounce) box chocolate cake mix
1 (14-ounce) package caramels, peeled
1 (5-ounce) can evaporated milk
½ (12-ounce) package chocolate chips
1 cup chopped nuts

Grease and flour a 9x13-inch baking pan. Mix cake according to directions on box. Spread ½ of batter into pan; bake 20 minutes in preheated 350° oven. In saucepan, melt caramels and milk together. Pour caramel mixture over hot cake; sprinkle chocolate chips and nuts over top. Spoon remaining ½ of batter over top and continue baking 25 minutes longer. Serves 12–15.

If you open one end of a can of evaporated milk (or any liquid) with an old-fashioned beer opener ("church key"), the milk may eventually come out if you shake it. But you must put a hole in the other side of the lid in order for it to pour. Now it's **fast**. (Bet you knew that.)

We must go **fast**, because the race is against time.

—Anna Held

Layer-By-Layer of Goodness

Pretty in a trifle bowl, too.

1 (6-ounce) package French vanilla instant pudding mix
3¾ cups milk
½ angel food cake, prepared
1 (8-ounce) carton sour cream
1 (21-ounce) can pie filling of choice

Whisk pudding mix with milk for 1 minute. Break cake into pieces in a 9x13-inch pan. Spread sour cream, then pudding, over cake; pour pie filling on top; chill. Serves 12–15.

Pudding Stack Cake

1 (6-ounce) package vanilla instant pudding
3 cups milk
1 (8-ounce) container Cool Whip
1 box graham crackers
1 (15-ounce) can chocolate fudge frosting

Make pudding using 3 cups milk; fold in Cool Whip. Place a layer of whole graham crackers in a 9x13-inch dish; add a layer of pudding. Alternate layers, ending with graham crackers. Heat frosting to spreadable texture and spread on top of graham crackers. Refrigerate. Serves 8–10.

Fast &

less time

Big Brickle Cake

1 (18¼-ounce) box butter cake mix
1 (14-ounce) can sweetened condensed milk
1 (12-ounce) jar caramel ice cream topping
1 (12-ounce) package brickle bits, divided
1 (16-ounce) carton Cool Whip

Bake cake as directed for 9x13-inch baking pan. Remove from oven, and while cake is still hot, poke holes in top with a fork. Combine sweetened condensed milk and caramel topping. Pour caramel mixture over cake. Sprinkle ½ of the brickle bits over top; cool. Cover with plastic wrap and refrigerate till cold.

Frost with Cool Whip. Sprinkle with remaining brickle bits. Serves 12–15.

Not-Too-Big Hot Milk Cake

2 eggs
1 cup sugar
1 cup self-rising flour
½ cup hot milk
1 teaspoon vanilla

Beat eggs till light and fluffy. Add sugar and mix well. Add sifted flour; mix well. Add hot milk and vanilla; mix well. Bake in greased 8x8-inch pan about 20 minutes, or till done. May be doubled for layer cake, or used for cupcakes, and frosted with your choice of icing. Serves 4–8.

Amaretto Angel Loaf

1 bought angel food loaf (or round) cake
8 tablespoons amaretto
3 cups vanilla ice cream
1 (12-ounce) carton Cool Whip

Split cake into 3 layers and place on plate or casserole dish. Drizzle first layer with 2 tablespoons amaretto; cover with a cup of ice cream; repeat with remaining two layers. Add remaining 2 tablespoons amaretto to Cool Whip and ice cake; freeze. Easy to serve because it does not freeze hard. Serves 8–12.

Almond Cookie Cake

These may be cut into small squares, diamonds, or in cookie-cutter shapes.

2 sticks butter, softened
2 cups all-purpose flour
2 cups sugar
5 eggs
8 ounces almonds, ground

Combine all ingredients in mixing bowl; beat on MEDIUM speed 6 minutes. Spread in a greased 10x15-inch jellyroll pan. Bake at 325° for 45 minutes till light brown. To serve, dust with powdered sugar, or a dollop of lemon curd. Serves 10–12.

Surprise Cake

Surprise! Cake bakes and makes a layer of cheese on the bottom.

1 (18¼-ounce) box butter cake mix
1 (16-ounce) carton ricotta cheese
¾ cup sugar
3 eggs
1½ teaspoons coconut extract

Prepare cake mix as directed on package; pour into a lightly greased 9x13-inch pan. Combine ricotta cheese, sugar, eggs, and extract in mixer. Pour over cake batter in pan. Bake at 350° for 30–35 minutes or till cake tests done. Sprinkle powdered sugar on top, if desired. Cool and refrigerate. Pretty to serve with strawberries. Serves 12–15.

Cool Coconut Cake

A great make-ahead dessert.

1 (18¼-ounce) box yellow cake mix
2 cups sugar
1 (8-ounce) carton sour cream
1 (12-ounce) package flaked coconut
2 cups Cool Whip

Prepare cake mix in 2 (9-inch) round pans as directed on package; cool, then split layers. Combine sugar, sour cream, and coconut, reserving 1 cup for later. Spread remaining mixture between layers. Mix reserved mixture with Cool Whip, then frost cake. Store in airtight container in refrigerator. Serves 15–20.

Fast Rising Yeast

This very active strain of yeast allows you to make bread with only one rise. Unlike ordinary active dry yeast, instant yeast doesn't need to be dissolved in liquid first—you just add it to the dry ingredients.

Fab & more taste

Butter Delight Pound Cake

3 sticks butter, softened
2½ cups powdered sugar
6 eggs
2½ cups all-purpose flour
1 teaspoon vanilla

Beat butter and sugar till creamy; add eggs, one at a time. Add flour to mixture gradually; add vanilla; blend well. Bake in greased and floured Bundt pan for 1 hour at 325°. Serves 10–12.

Ten-Egg Butter Pound Cake

1 pound butter, softened
3 cups sugar
1½ teaspoons vanilla flavoring
3 cups all-purpose flour
10 large eggs

Mix one stick butter at a time with sugar, beating after each; add vanilla. Alternate blending flour and 1 egg at a time into mixture. Pour into a greased and floured Bundt or tube pan. Bake 1½ hours at 325°. Serves 10–12.

Chocolate-Chocolate Pound Cake

1 (18¼-ounce) package chocolate cake mix
1 (3-ounce) box chocolate instant pudding mix
1 cup milk
¾ cup oil
4 eggs, beaten

Mix cake and pudding mix in large bowl. Mix in milk, oil, and eggs; beat well. Pour into greased and floured tube pan and bake at 350° for 1 hour. Serves 10–12.

Yogurt Cheesecake Cups

2 (8-ounce) packages cream cheese, softened
2 tablespoons honey
2 (6-ounce) cartons cherry or cranberry yogurt
12–16 chocolate- or vanilla-filled cookies
Sliced maraschino cherries for garnish

Beat cream cheese, honey, and yogurt till fluffy. Place a cookie in paper cup liners in regular muffin tin; top with creamed mixture; chill at least 1 hour. Garnish with cherries. Add a dollop of whipped cream, if desired. Makes 12–16.

Lickety-Split Lemon Cheesecake

1 (8-ounce) package cream cheese, softened
2 cups milk, divided
1 (3-ounce) package lemon instant pudding mix
1 (8-inch) graham cracker crust

Beat cream cheese with ½ cup milk. Mix in remaining milk and pudding mix till well mixed, about 1 minute (do not overbeat). Pour into crust; chill at least 1 hour. Garnish with lemon curls or lemon zest and mint leaves, if desired. Serves 6–8.

Cheesecake Tarts

½ cup sour cream
½ (8-ounce) package cream cheese, softened
2 tablespoons sugar
1 teaspoon vanilla
2 (2.1-ounce) packages frozen miniature phyllo
  shells, thawed

Combine sour cream, cream cheese, sugar, and vanilla; mix well. Spoon into phyllo shells. Chill until serving. May top with fruit or pie filling of choice, if desired. Serves 4–8.

Superb Cupcake Cheesecakes

3 (8-ounce) packages cream cheese, softened
5 eggs
1½ teaspoons vanilla
1¼ cups sugar, divided
1 (8-ounce) carton sour cream

Beat cream cheese till fluffy; add eggs, one at a time. Add vanilla and 1 cup sugar; mix well. Pour into 24 paper-lined cupcake tins; bake at 300° for 20 minutes. Meanwhile mix sour cream and remaining ¼ cup sugar. Spoon mixture on each cupcake and bake 6 minutes longer. Cool, then refrigerate. Makes 2 dozen.

More **Fast**
and
Fabulous

FIVE ★ STAR

Cookies & Candies

Simple Shortbread Cookies

2 sticks butter, softened
¾ cup sugar
2¼ cups all-purpose flour

Mix butter and sugar thoroughly. Add flour, ½ cup at a time, mixing until crumbly. Knead until smooth. Press evenly on cookie sheet; bake at 325° for 20–25 minutes. Cut into squares while hot.

Editor's Extra: Fun to use a cookie stamp on these before baking.

Lemon-Glazed Shortbread Cookies

2 sticks butter, softened
2 cups powdered sugar, divided
1¼ cups all-purpose flour
¾ cup cornstarch
3 tablespoons lemon juice (or orange)

Cream butter and ½ cup sugar well. Beat in flour and cornstarch. Cover and refrigerate at least 2 hours or overnight.

Roll dough into 1-inch balls. Place on ungreased cookie sheet; bake at 325° for 10 minutes. Cool slightly, then remove from pan; cool on brown or parchment paper. Paint cookies with a glaze of remaining 1½ cups powdered sugar mixed with orange or lemon juice. Makes 3½ dozen cookies.

Shortbread Wedges

Have a slice!

1 stick butter, softened
⅓ cup brown sugar, packed
¾ cup plus 2 tablespoons all-purpose flour
¼ teaspoon cinnamon
⅔ cup quick oats

Cream butter and sugar until light and fluffy. Sift flour and cinnamon into bowl with oats. Add to creamed mixture, mixing just until combined. Press into ungreased pie tin. Bake at 350° for 40 minutes. Mark in wedges when just out of oven. Cool; break into wedges. Makes 8–10 wedges.

Editor's Extra: A great base for fruits, puddings, mousses, ice cream . . . in a serving dish or to stick a thin wedge alongside.

Almond Sandies

2 sticks butter, softened
1 cup powdered sugar, divided
1 cup finely chopped almonds
1½ teaspoons almond extract
2 cups all-purpose flour

Cream butter and ¾ cup powdered sugar; add nuts, almond extract, and flour; mix well. Chill dough; roll into balls. Bake on ungreased cookie sheet at 350° for 20 minutes. Cool; then roll in remaining ¼ cup powdered sugar to coat. Makes about 3 dozen.

Crackle-Top Chocolate Cookies

Soft cookies with crackle-y tops.

1 (8-ounce) package cream cheese, softened
½ cup butter, softened
1 egg
1 teaspoon vanilla
1 (18¼-ounce) box chocolate cake mix

Cream together cream cheese and butter; add egg and vanilla, beating well. Add cake mix and mix well. Refrigerate, covered, 1 or 2 hours. Roll into walnut-size balls. Place 2 inches apart on ungreased cookie sheet; bake 10–12 minutes at 350° or until tops crack. Cool slightly in pan before moving to cooling rack. Makes 2–3 dozen.

Editor's Extra: These can be made with other flavors of cake mixes as well.

Fly-Away Butter Cookies

These are so light and delicate. Pretty for the holidays.

2 sticks butter, softened
¾ cup powdered sugar
1¾ cups all-purpose flour
1½ teaspoons extract (almond, peppermint,
  vanilla, or coconut)
Colored sugar

Cream butter and sugar; gradually mix in flour; add extract of choice. Roll into small balls and put on ungreased cookie sheet 1 inch apart. Color sugar red or green for Christmas, yellow or blue or purple for Easter, or create your team's colors (about ¼ cup sugar with a few drops of food coloring shaken in a plastic bag). Flatten each cookie ball with the bottom of a damp glass dipped in the sugar. Bake in 350° oven 12–14 minutes till firm. Cool on wire racks. Makes about 4 dozen.

Kids-Love-To-Make-These Peanut Butter Cookies

1 cup crunchy peanut butter
1 egg
1 cup sugar
1 teaspoon baking soda
1 teaspoon vanilla

Mix all ingredients thoroughly. Drop by teaspoonfuls onto baking pan; press with fork. Bake 10–12 minutes at 350°. Cool before removing from pan. Makes 24–30 cookies.

Fingernails grow nearly four times **faster** than toenails. Your middle fingernail grows the **fastest**.

Peanut Butter Crunchies

5 slices bread
2–3 tablespoons vegetable oil
½ cup crunchy peanut butter

Cut crusts from bread and reserve; cut bread into strips. Spread both out on baking sheet, and toast at 225° till crisp (80 minutes). Put just the crusts in food processor to make fine crumbs; set aside. Mix oil and peanut butter to make a thick liquid. Dip each strip in mixture and roll in crumbs. Drain on paper towels or baking racks. Keep in cookie tin. Makes 15–20.

Fastest Roller Coaster in the World

Formula Rossa at Ferrari World on Yas Island in Abu Dhabi, United Arab Emirates has a hydraulic launch coaster, and blasts from 0–62 miles in just 2 seconds, and goes 149.1 mph in 4.9 seconds. It is said to give you the feeling of racing in a real Formula 1 Car. They provide the goggles and helmets; you provide the screams.

Quick Coconut Cocoons

2 egg whites
½ teaspoon almond extract
½ cup sugar
1 cup shredded coconut

Whip egg whites with almond extract to soft peaks. Slowly add sugar while beating to soft peaks; do not beat stiff. Fold in coconut and drop by heaping teaspoon onto well-greased baking pan. Bake at 325° for 20 minutes. Makes 24 cookies.

Simply Coconut Macaroons

For coconut lovers.

⅔ cup sweetened condensed milk
1 egg white
1½ teaspoons vanilla
⅛ teaspoon salt
3½ cups flaked or shredded sweetened coconut

Mix first 4 ingredients together; stir in coconut till well mixed. Drop by heaping teaspoonfuls onto parchment-lined cookie sheets. Bake at 350° for 20–25 minutes till nicely browned. Leave on paper till completely cool, then peel off. Makes about 24 cookies.

Coconut Macaroon Fingers

10 bread slices, crusts trimmed, cut into fingers
1 (14-ounce) can sweetened condensed milk
1 cup shredded coconut

Dip bread fingers into milk, coating all sides; immediately roll into coconut. Bake at 350° till very lightly browned. Makes 30–40 fingers.

Editor's Extra: Tint coconut by shaking in a zipper bag with a few drops of food coloring to match the occasion.

Red Velvet Moon Pies

Grandkids love to make 'em and eat 'em . . . and laugh at their red fingers.

1 (18¼-ounce) box red velvet cake mix
1 stick butter, softened
2 eggs, beaten
1 (15-ounce) can cream cheese frosting

Combine dry cake mix, butter, and eggs well. Drop by teaspoon onto parchment-paper-lined cookie sheet, then flatten each cookie. Bake at 350° for 8–10 minutes. Cool; spread cream cheese icing between 2 cookies. Makes about 60 cookies (30 filled moon pies).

Editor's Extra: Delicious to add ¾ cup mini chocolate chips to half the batter; spread icing on plain cookies, frost, then put a chocolate chip cookie on top.

Raspberry-Filled Finger Pastries

½ (8-ounce) package cream cheese, softened
1 stick butter, softened
1 cup all-purpose flour, sifted
½ cup seedless raspberry jam
Powdered sugar

Mix cream cheese, butter, and flour well. Chill. Roll out dough onto floured surface to ¼-inch thickness. Cut into 2-inch squares. Put ½ teaspoon of jam on each square. Bring 2 corners up to meet in middle, then 2 opposite corners, and crimp. Bake on ungreased cookie sheets at 350° for 20 minutes, till lightly browned. Cool, then sprinkle with powdered sugar. Makes 2 dozen or more.

Praline Crackers

A hands-down favorite!

½ box graham crackers
½ cup chopped almonds or pecans
2 sticks butter
½ cup sugar

Break crackers at perforations and place side by side on cookie sheet with sides. Sprinkle nuts over crackers. Cook butter and sugar in saucepan, 2–3 minutes until sugar is melted. Pour sugar mixture over crackers and nuts. Bake in 325° oven 20 minutes. Remove immediately to brown or wax paper to cool. Makes about 30.

Nutty Wafers

1 cup sugar
1 cup all-purpose flour
1 stick butter, softened
1 egg, separated
½ cup grated pecans

Mix sugar, flour, and butter like biscuit dough; add egg yolk; mix well. Divide dough into 6–8 pieces and pat onto greased cookie sheet to cover pan. Beat egg white slightly and rub over dough. Sprinkle with nuts. Bake at 275° about 30 minutes; mark cookies into squares or wedges. Put back in oven for 5 minutes. Remove from pan as soon as you take them out of oven. Makes 24.

Chocolate Chip Buttercups

An oldie, but goodie.

1 roll refrigerated chocolate chip cookie dough
**1 (12-ounce) package mini Reese's Peanut
  Butter Cups**

Slice dough in 1-inch slices, then cut in quarters. Place each quarter in lightly greased miniature muffin tins. Bake 8 minutes at 350°. Unwrap peanut butter cups and press into center of each cookie so that cookie dough is around sides. Bake another 5–7 minutes till browned on edges. Let cool. Makes 24–32.

Bryce's Favorite Cookie Bars

These are awesome! —Bryce Moseley (Barbara's teenage grandson)

1 (18¼-ounce) box yellow cake mix
1 stick butter, melted
3 eggs, divided
1 (1-pound) box powdered sugar
1 (8-ounce) package cream cheese, softened

Mix cake mix, butter, and 1 egg; press into 9x13-inch pan. Mix remaining 2 eggs, sugar, and cream cheese; beat 3 minutes. Pour cheese mixture over cake mixture; bake at 325° for 35–40 minutes. Allow to cool completely before cutting. Makes 20–24 bars.

Editor's Extra: Sprinkle with chopped nuts, coconut, or additional powdered sugar as soon as you remove from oven, if desired.

Fastest Crossing of the English Channel by Amphibious Vehicle

In 2004, all it took for Sir Richard Branson of the UK to drive a street-legal Gibbs Aquada between Dover, UK, and Calais, France, was one hour, forty minutes, and six seconds.

The **fastest** circum-navigation of the globe by car was accomplished in 1989 by Saloo and Neena Choudhury of India. The journey took 69 days, 19 hours, and 5 minutes, covering six continents and 24,901 road miles.

Spice Cookie Bars

1 (18¼-ounce) box spice cake mix
⅔ cup shortening
3 eggs, beaten
1 cup raisins
1 cup chopped nuts

Mix first 3 ingredients together well; mix in raisins and nuts. Smooth into greased 9x13-inch pan. Bake in 350° oven 25–30 minutes. Cut into bars when cool. Makes 18–24.

Cocoa Mallow Bites

½ (10-ounce) bag large marshmallows
1 (8-ounce) packages caramels, peeled
1 stick butter
½ (14-ounce) can sweetened condensed milk
½ (10-ounce) box cocoa crispy rice cereal

Cut marshmallows in half and freeze. Melt caramels, butter, and milk in double boiler. Dip marshmallows in mixture and roll in cereal. Refrigerate to set. Makes 4 dozen.

Chocolate Peanut Butter Crispies

1 (16-ounce) jar peanut butter
1 (1-pound) box powdered sugar
1 stick butter, melted
3 cups crispy rice cereal
2 cups semisweet chocolate chips, melted

In large mixing bowl, blend peanut butter and sugar; add melted butter and continue to blend. Stir in cereal; toss to coat well. Spread mixture in a lightly greased 9x13-inch pan. Spread melted chocolate evenly over cereal layer. Refrigerate to cool; cut into bars. Makes 30 bars.

Over-The-Top Dessert

1 (21-ounce) box fudge brownie mix
1 (8-ounce) package cream cheese, softened
½ cup powdered sugar
10 strawberries, stemmed, sliced

Mix brownies according to package directions; spread in a greased pizza pan. Bake at 350° for 17–20 minutes; cool slightly.

Beat cream cheese with powdered sugar till smooth. Dollop all over baked brownies, then spread carefully over top. Bake 10 minutes more at 350°. Cool, then put strawberry slices all over top. Cut into wedges. Serves 8–10. Refrigerate leftovers.

Editor's Extra: Add a squirt or dollop of whipped cream, and you've definitely got an over-the-top dessert!

Cookie Sundaes

My daughter Heather makes a big skillet while the kids' slumber party is going on, then calls them in! She has newspaper spread on the table with a towel under and over the handle of the hot skillet, and a long iced tea spoon for each kid to dive in! Always a hit! —Gwen McKee

1 bag chocolate chip cookie mix
Vanilla ice cream
Chocolate syrup
Whipped cream or topping

Mix cookie mix according to directions on package and spread into 1 (12-inch) or 2 (7-inch) iron skillets. Bake at 350° per package directions. Serve slices hot with ice cream. Drizzle with chocolate syrup and top with lots of whipped cream or topping. Maraschino cherries on top make it extra special. Serves 6–10.

Editor's Extra: Sub different flavors of ice cream.

Fab *more taste*

Christmas Wreaths

1 stick butter, cut in pieces
1 teaspoon vanilla
2 teaspoons green food coloring
3 cups miniature marshmallows
3½ cups cornflakes

Melt butter in saucepan; add vanilla, food coloring, and marshmallows. Cook on low heat, stirring constantly, till melted. Remove from heat and gradually stir in cornflakes. Drop by teaspoonfuls onto wax paper. Butter hands and shape into small wreaths. Decorate with red cinnamon drop candies or red sprinkles, if desired. Makes about 30 (2-inch) wreaths.

Noodle-In-A-Haystack Cookies

2 (12-ounce) packages chocolate or butter-scotch chips
1 (12-ounce) package chow mein noodles

Melt chocolate chips in 2 batches for 2 minutes (butterscotch 1½) in microwave on HIGH; stir. Pour over chow mein noodles in large bowl. Stir gently till all are coated. With large fork, place on wax paper. Makes about 30.

Cocoa Nut Nuggets

1½ cups Cocoa Krispies
1½ cups Captain Crunch Peanut Butter Cereal
1½ cups dry-roasted peanuts
1 (16-ounce) package chocolate candy coating

Combine cereal and nuts in large bowl. Melt chocolate in microwave 2 minutes; stir. Pour cereal mixture into chocolate; stir well to coat all; drop by teaspoonfuls onto wax paper. Makes about 60.

Editor's Extra: Fun to use pastel colors of white chocolate.

Fruit Flake Turtles

1 pound milk chocolate
15 caramels
5 cups cornflakes
1 cup chopped nuts
1 cup dried fruit bits

Melt chocolate and caramels; add cornflakes, nuts, and fruit bits. Mix lightly till all is coated; drop by teaspoon onto wax paper. Let set until firm. Makes about 24.

Fast Pokey Turtles

2 cups semisweet chocolate chips
1 (12-ounce) package caramels, peeled
¾ (12-ounce) package peanut butter chips
2 cups pecan halves, divided

In microwave oven, melt chocolate chips 2 minutes on HIGH in 4- or 8-cup glass measure; stir.

In large Pam-sprayed pan, partially melt caramels on low-medium heat; add peanut butter chips; mix thoroughly. Add ¾ of the pecans to caramel/peanut butter mixture.

On parchment paper, for each turtle, spoon chocolate, then caramel mixture, then chocolate, and top with a pecan. Allow to set. Makes about 40.

Two turtles crossing the road hit each other head-on and were both knocked unconscious. The policeman who was summoned to investigate found a snail nearby who had witnessed the accident.

"Can you tell me what happened?" the officer asked.

"Yes, I saw it," replied the snail, "but it all happened so **fast**!"

Almond Angels

3 egg whites
2¼ cups sugar
1½ cups all-purpose flour
1 cup ground almonds

Beat egg whites on high speed until frothy; beat in sugar a little at a time till somewhat stiff. Lower speed and add flour gradually; fold in almonds. Drop by spoonfuls onto greased cookie sheet. Bake at 350° for 13–15 minutes till their color changes. Makes 30 or more.

Editor's Extra: Add a drop of food coloring to match the season or your party theme, if desired.

Light Bite Meringues

4 large egg whites, room temperature
3½ cups sifted powdered sugar, divided
2 teaspoons cherry Jell-O
1 teaspoon white vinegar
1 cup mini chocolate chips (optional)

Preheat oven to 300°. Line cookie sheet with parchment paper. In a glass or copper bowl, with an electric mixer, beat egg whites and 2 cups sugar together until smooth. Beat in remaining sugar and Jell-O till stiff peaks form. Drop by teaspoonfuls onto lined cookie sheet, about an inch apart. Bake, rotating cookie sheets once or twice, for about 1 hour, or until meringues are firm and completely dry. Remove from parchment paper and let cool completely on wire racks. Makes 48 or more.

White Cloud Meringues

4 egg whites
1 teaspoon vanilla
½ teaspoon vinegar
1 cup sugar

Beat egg whites till frothy; add vanilla, vinegar, and a dash of salt while beating to soft peaks. Add sugar gradually while continuing to beat till stiff. Drop by tablespoonfuls onto parchment-lined pans; bake 45–60 minutes. Cool on racks. Makes about 24.

Editor's Extra: These are easy to shape into meringue cups by making a little hole in the middle of each meringue with a spoon before baking. When ready to serve, put a little seedless raspberry preserves in center. Or melt chocolate chips with just a tad of hot water, and when cool, fold in some whipped topping.

Space Rocks

3 cups powdered sugar
⅔ cup unsweetened cocoa powder
2¾ cups chopped toasted pecans
4 large egg whites, room temperature
1 teaspoon almond extract

Preheat oven to 350°. Whisk powdered sugar with cocoa powder and a pinch of salt in a large bowl. Whisk in chopped pecans. Add egg whites and almond extract; beat one minute—no more. Spoon batter in 24 rounded mounds onto baking sheets covered with parchment paper. Bake 20 minutes, or until tops are glossy and firm. Slide parchment paper off hot cookie sheet. Carefully peel parchment from cookies when cool. Makes about 48.

Pecan Pie Cookies

Tastes just like a pecan pie in a cookie...just easier to serve.

1 stick butter, softened
1 cup firmly packed dark brown sugar
1 egg
1 cup all-purpose flour
1 cup chopped pecans

Mix all together; spoon onto ungreased baking pans; bake in 375° oven 12–15 minutes or until brown around edges. Cool 2 minutes in pans, then 10 minutes on rack to cool completely. Makes 24 big, or 36 small tea cookies.

Orange Candy-Coated Pecans

2 cups sugar
1 cup water
1 tablespoon orange juice
1½ teaspoons grated orange rind
3 cups chopped pecans

Cook sugar and water to soft-ball stage (235°). Add juice and rind and beat till it begins to thicken; add pecans. Stir till sugar coated. Dip onto wax paper. Makes about 24.

Debberino's Pecan Zappers

This will become your favorite candy as soon as you taste one. Make them for favorite clients—keeps them coming back.
—Debbie Wedgeworth

1½ cups pecan halves
⅓ (24-ounce) package chocolate almond bark (4 blocks)
⅓ cup raisins

Spread pecan halves onto a large paper plate or platter. Microwave on HIGH 2 minutes. Stir and microwave 2 minutes more. Cool. Microwave chocolate 2 minutes on HIGH in 8-cup glass measure; stir till smooth. Stir in raisins and cooled pecans till all are covered well. Spoon onto a strip of parchment or wax paper into clusters. Allow to set an hour or so. Makes 20–25. Store in a tin.

Editor's Extra: Debbie sometimes stirs a tablespoon or so of melted butter onto the pecans before microwaving, but be careful not to burn them. And of course, you can toast them in the oven as well.

Easy Millionaires

2 (14-ounce) packages vanilla caramels
1 tablespoon evaporated milk
1 cup semisweet chocolate chips
⅓ bar paraffin
8 cups chopped pecans

Melt first 4 ingredients over medium heat in heavy saucepan; stir in pecans. Drop onto greased wax paper; cool. Makes 4 dozen or more.

Fastest Time on a Treadmill

Arulanantham Suresh Joachim of Sri Lanka ran 100 miles on a treadmill in 3 hours, 42 minutes, and 33 seconds.

Pecan Butter Balls

1 cup butter, softened
¼ cup sugar
1 tablespoon vanilla
2 cups all-purpose flour, sifted
2 cups finely ground pecans

Cream butter and sugar; add vanilla. Stir in flour and ground pecans. Roll into small balls; place on greased cookie sheets. Bake in 300° oven 45 minutes. While hot, roll in powdered sugar, if desired, then again when cold. Makes 3–4 dozen.

Chinese Chocolate Nuggets

½ (12-ounce) package butterscotch chips
½ (12-ounce) package chocolate chips
1 cup Chinese noodles
1 cup dry roasted peanuts

Melt chips together in microwave on HIGH 1½ minutes; stir; zap 15–30 seconds more till melted; mix till smooth. Add noodles and peanuts and mix until coated. Drop by teaspoonfuls onto wax paper; let set till firm. Makes about 30.

Peanut Butter Toads

1 pound white chocolate
1 cup peanut butter
2 cups honey-roasted peanuts
2 cups crispy rice cereal
2 cups miniature marshmallows

Melt white chocolate and peanut butter together in double boiler or microwave. Add remaining ingredients and stir to mix; drop onto wax paper on cookie sheet. Cool. Makes a lot!

Tart and Sweet Fruit Bites

Great for holidays and cookie exchanges.

1 (16-ounce) package dried apricots
1 (14-ounce) can sweetened condensed milk
1 teaspoon vanilla
1 (16-ounce) package shredded coconut

Finely grind apricots in food processor; add sweetened condensed milk and vanilla. Roll into small balls, then roll in coconut. These keep several weeks in an airtight container. Makes about 24.

Crazy Craisin Candy

½ (24-ounce) package almond bark
1 (12-ounce) package craisins

In microwave, melt almond bark; drop craisins into melted bark, a few at a time. Spoon onto wax paper, individually, to dry. Makes 20–25.

Editor's Extra: If a recipe calls for 1 cup of cranberries, you should use ¾ cup of craisins. No need to "plump" in water. Craisins are ready to "plop" right in your mouth.

Nutty Fruit Balls

Great for snacks . . . anytime, anywhere.

1 (7-ounce) package dried fruit bits
½ cup chopped nuts
½ cup sesame seeds
½ cup shredded coconut
½ teaspoon grated orange rind (optional)

Process all ingredients in food processor. Roll into 1-inch balls. Store in zipper bag. Makes about 30.

Peanut Butter Candy Roll

1 (15-ounce) can white icing
1 (1-pound) box powdered sugar
½ teaspoon vanilla
1 cup creamy peanut butter

Cream icing in mixer; gradually add all but 2 table-spoons powdered sugar; cover and refrigerate 1 hour or more. Mix vanilla into peanut butter. Dust 2 (1-foot-long pieces of wax paper with remaining powdered sugar; place icing between the two sheets and roll with rolling pin to ¼-inch thickness. Remove top wax paper and spread peanut butter on top of icing; roll up jellyroll style. Cut into 6–8 sections and cover top with wax paper to firm in refrigerator.

Choco-Peanut Butter Breaks

8 ounces white candy coating, chopped
1 cup semisweet chocolate chips
¾ cup peanut butter

In separate bowls, melt white and chocolate candy 2 minutes each on HIGH. Stir peanut butter into the white candy coating; pour onto parchment or wax-paper-lined cookie sheet. Drizzle sparsely with chocolate; swirl through with a table knife—don't overswirl; you want it to be distinctly white and chocolate. Chill. Break into pieces when firm. Store covered in refrigerator. Makes 20–30 pieces.

Editor's Extra: Good with crunchy peanut butter, too.

Crème de Menthe Bon Bons

2 sticks butter, softened
2 pounds powdered sugar, divided
⅓ cup crème de menthe
¼ block paraffin
2 cups semisweet chocolate chips

Cream butter with all but ¾ cup sugar, along with a pinch of salt, and crème de menthe. Roll into small balls; roll balls in reserved powdered sugar. Refrigerate till firm.

   Melt paraffin in double boiler; slowly add chocolate. Keep on lowest heat. Dip balls in chocolate with toothpick. Place on wax paper on pan; refrigerate. If necessary, thin chocolate with a few drops of oil. Makes over 100 balls.

Editor's Extra: Add a few drops of green food coloring, if deeper green is desired.

Lance Armstrong bicycled at an average speed of 25.026 mph in the 1999 Tour de France.

Cool Pistachio Balls

These are cool and delicious. —Betty Harris

3 tablespoons baking cocoa
1 (14-ounce) can sweetened condensed milk
2 tablespoons butter
1 cup shelled pistachios, finely chopped

Bring cocoa, milk, and butter to boil, stirring constantly. Reduce heat to low; cook and stir until thickened. Transfer to small bowl. Cover and refrigerate until chilled. Roll into 1-inch balls; roll in pistachios. Store in refrigerator. Makes 2½ dozen.

Fastest Time up the Steps of the Empire State Building

There are 1,576 steps to the top of the Empire State Building in New York City. Paul Crake of Australia ran up in 9 minutes and 33 seconds.

Christmas Cherry Bark

Pretty and popular.

1 (12-ounce) package vanilla chips
6 ounces white candy coating, chopped
½ cup chopped dried cherries
½ cup chopped almonds or pistachios

Microwave chips and candy coating on HIGH 1½ minutes; stir and continue at 15-second intervals until melted. Stir in cherries and nuts. Spread into a foil-lined 9x13-inch pan; refrigerate 20 minutes; score to later cut in square or diamond shapes. Refrigerate another 45 minutes till set. Cut and store in airtight container in refrigerator. Makes 24–30.

Editor's Extra: You may use all candy coating, if desired.

Heavenly Amaretto Fudge

2 cups sugar
⅓ cup amaretto liqueur
1 cup half-and-half

Combine all in large saucepan; stir over medium heat till sugar is dissolved. Bring to a boil and cook without stirring till soft-ball stage (235°). Remove from heat and cool down to 140°. Beat with spoon till mixture begins to thicken; pour quickly into buttered 8-inch pan. Cut when cool and hard. Makes 16–25.

Editor's Extra: One-half cup chopped pecans added after soft-ball stage could be heavenly-er.

Creamy Peanut Butter Fudge

2 cups sugar
½ cup light corn syrup
½ cup evaporated milk
¼ teaspoon salt
1 cup creamy peanut butter

Cook and stir sugar, syrup, milk, and salt in saucepan till it reaches soft-ball stage (235°). Cool 10 minutes; add peanut butter and beat well. Pour into buttered 8x8-inch pan. Cut into squares.

Cracker Jack Caramel Corn

½ cup white Karo syrup
2 cups brown sugar
1 cup salted butter
1 teaspoon baking soda
6–7 cups popped popcorn

Bring first 3 ingredients to a boil, and allow to boil for 5 minutes. Remove from heat and add baking soda. Spread popcorn in large roasting pan, and pour caramel mixture over top; stir with wooden spoon to mix well. Bake at 225° for 45 minutes, turning every 15 minutes to make sure it's evenly coated.

Ready-In-A-Snap Peanut Brittle

3 cups sugar
1 (8-ounce) jar salted dry-roasted peanuts
½ teaspoon baking soda

Cook sugar over low heat until melted and golden brown, stirring constantly. Add peanuts; mix well. Stir in baking soda (it will foam). Spread on baking sheet. Let cool; break into pieces.

Almond Brittle

1 stick butter
1 cup blanched slivered almonds
½ cup sugar
1 tablespoon light corn syrup

Line bottom and sides of an 8- or 9-inch cake pan with foil. Boil all ingredients in skillet over medium heat, stirring constantly till golden brown, about 6 minutes. Quickly spread in pan. Cool, then break into bite-size pieces. Makes about 20 pieces.

Praline Brittle

½ cup packed brown sugar
1½ cups sugar
1 (5-ounce) can evaporated milk
2 teaspoons vanilla
1 cup pecan pieces

Boil sugars, milk, and a dash of salt in heavy pot over medium-high heat, stirring continuously. Cook till a drop in ½ cup of water holds together (soft-ball stage—235°). Stir in vanilla and pecans. Pour onto buttered wax paper; cool. Break in pieces to serve.

Chocolate Pecan Brittle

1 pound butter
1 (1-pound) box light brown sugar
1 cup chopped pecans
1½ cups milk chocolate chips

Bring butter and sugar to a boil in heavy saucepan and cook to hard-crack stage (300° on candy thermometer), stirring occasionally. Grease 10x15-inch jellyroll pan and sprinkle with pecans. Pour sugar mixture over chopped pecans. Melt chocolate chips 2 minutes in microwave on HIGH; stir to smooth; spread over pecans. Allow to cool; break into pieces.

Marble Slab English Toffee

2 cups milk chocolate chips
⅔ cup water
1⅔ cups sugar
2 sticks butter
1½ cups chopped pecans

Melt chocolate in microwave 2 minutes; do not stir. Boil water, sugar, and butter in big heavy saucepan on medium-high heat till it reaches 280°. Add ½ the chopped nuts and stir constantly till it reaches 310°. Pour thinly onto ungreased marble slab (or silicone mat or parchment paper on cool surface) and spread with spatula; spread half the chocolate on one side; immediately sprinkle with ½ the remaining nuts, and pat lightly. Run spatula under candy and turn over; spread and pat this side with remaining chocolate and pecans. When cool, loosen from marble and break into pieces. Makes about 30.

Nutty Toffee Breaks

Have a "break" on your coffee break!

2 sticks butter
1 cup sugar
1 cup toasted sliced almonds, divided
1½ cups semisweet chocolate chips

Butter a 9x13-inch pan with a small amount of the butter. Cook and stir remaining butter and sugar over medium-high heat to soft-boil stage (240°). Stir in ½ cup almonds; pour into prepared pan. Sprinkle evenly with chocolate chips. When glossy, spread chocolate over top lightly. Sprinkle remaining almonds over top. Refrigerate till set. Break into pieces. Store in airtight container. Makes 24–30.

Fastest Talker

Canadian Sean Shannon recited Hamlet's soliloquy (260 words) in 23.8 seconds. Whew! That's 655 words a minute.

Make-Your-Own Butter Mints

Nice to have on hand, and to bring to friends.

2 tablespoons butter
½ (8-ounce) package cream cheese
1 (1-pound) box powdered sugar
⅛ teaspoon vanilla extract
¼ teaspoon peppermint extract

Melt butter and cream cheese in large saucepan over low heat; stir to mix. Gradually stir in powdered sugar till smooth; add vanilla and peppermint. Divide mixture into 10 (¼-cup) portions; roll each into a 12-inch rope. Cut into ½-inch pieces. Let stand, uncovered, till firm, 3–5 hours.

Editor's Extra: Add a drop of food coloring if you want pastel mints.

No-Bake Pastel Mints

1 (3-ounce) package cream cheese, softened
¼ cup all-vegetable shortening
½ teaspoon peppermint oil
1 (1-pound) box powdered sugar
Food coloring (optional)

Mix first three ingredients, then add powdered sugar and mix well. Add food coloring of choice, if desired. Roll into small balls and place on wax-paper or parchment-paper-lined baking pan. Flatten each ball with bottom of a cup. Chill, covered with plastic wrap, until ready to serve. Makes 50–60 mints.

More **Fast** **and** **Fabulous**

FIVE ★ STAR

Pies & Other Desserts

Easy Peachy Pie

4 cups peeled, thinly sliced fresh peaches
1 cup sugar
1 cup self-rising flour
1 egg, beaten
1 stick butter, melted

Place sliced peaches in a greased 8x8-inch baking pan. Mix sugar, flour, and egg till crumbly. Put on top of peaches. Pour melted butter over top. Bake at 375° for 30–35 minutes, until brown and bubbly. Serves 6.

Editor's Extra: If eggs are small, use two.

Fried Peach Pies

2 cups all-purpose flour
1 teaspoon salt
½ cup cold butter
½ cup cold water
1 cup mashed sweetened peaches

Sift flour and salt together; cut in cold butter and mix with hands; add water. Roll ⅛ inch thick between wax paper. Cut with large cookie cutter about 4 inches in diameter. In each round, place 1½ tablespoons mashed peaches. Moisten edges with water; fold over and press edges together with fork. Fry in hot deep oil till golden. Drain on paper towels. May sprinkle with powdered sugar, if desired. Makes about 8 pies.

Editor's Extra: A tiny bit of almond extract in with the sweetened peaches is *very* nice indeed.

Judy's Frozen Lemon Pie

A light dessert that is easy to make and handy to have in the freezer. —Judy Tyler

1 (12-ounce) can evaporated milk
1 cup sugar
Juice of 2 lemons, plus zest of one
1 graham cracker crust

Put can of evaporated milk in freezer for 45 minutes. Whip till somewhat stiff; gradually whip in sugar. Fold juice and zest into mixture. Pour into crust; cover with plastic wrap; freeze. Serves 8.

Nancy's Lemon Pie

Great and refreshing dessert for summer. —Nancy Seale

1 (6-ounce) can frozen lemonade, thawed
1 (8-ounce) carton Cool Whip, thawed
1 (14-ounce) can sweetened condensed milk
1 graham cracker pie crust

Mix first 3 ingredients well and pour into pie crust. Chill well before serving. Serves 8.

Make-In-Minutes Lemon Cream Pie

1 (14-ounce) can sweetened condensed milk
1 (8-ounce) package cream cheese, softened
¼ cup lemon juice
1 (21-ounce) can lemon pie filling
1 (9-inch) graham cracker pie crust

Combine sweetened condensed milk, cream cheese, and lemon juice; beat till smooth. Fold in lemon pie filling. Pour mixture into pie crust; refrigerate several hours before serving. Serves 8.

Easy Piña Colada Pie

This is too good to be so simple. —Courtney Jernigan

1 (10-ounce) can frozen piña colada mix
1 (12-ounce) carton whipped cream cheese
1 (16-ounce) carton whipped topping, divided
1 graham cracker pie crust

Whip piña colada mix and cream cheese till well combined. Fold in 1½ cups whipped topping. Pour mixture into pie crust and top with remaining whipped topping. Serves 8.

Editor's Extra: May add ½ cup flaked coconut and crushed pineapple to mix, if desired. To make Lemonade or Limeade Pie, just sub lemonade or limeade concentrate for the piña colada mix.

Nutty Ritzy Pie

4 egg whites
1 cup sugar
½ teaspoon baking powder
18 Ritz Crackers, crumbled
¼ cup chopped pecans

Beat egg whites till foamy. Add sugar and baking powder to egg whites. Beat till stiff peaks form. Fold in cracker crumbs and pecans. Bake in buttered 9-inch pie pan 45 minutes at 300°. Cool. Garnish with extra cracker crumbs and pecans. Serves 6–8.

Editor's Extra: Serve with whipped cream, if desired.

It's-A-Melody-In-Your-Mouth Tartlets

Everybody sings their praises.

1 (16.5-ounce) tube refrigerator sugar cookie dough
1 (8-ounce) package cream cheese, softened
1 cup powdered sugar
2–3 tablespoons Amaretto liqueur (or flavoring of choice)
24 raspberries (or blueberries or strawberry halves)

Heat oven to 350°. Grease or spray 24 mini muffin cups. Cut cookie dough into 24 squares. Press 1 square in bottom and up side of each mini muffin cups. Bake 10–15 minutes or until edges are deep golden brown. Cool 5 minutes. With tip of handle of wooden spoon, press dough down in center of each cup to make room for 1–2 tablespoons filling. Top each with 1 raspberry or other small fruit.

Creamy Chocolate Pie

1 (8-ounce) package cream cheese, softened
1 cup milk
1 (3-ounce) package chocolate instant pudding mix
1 (8-ounce) carton Cool Whip, divided
1 (9-inch) graham cracker crust

Beat cream cheese till smooth, adding milk a little at a time. Add pudding mix and beat till smooth. Mix in ¾ of Cool Whip. Pour into pie shell and refrigerate 2–3 hours, till set. Garnish with dollops of remaining Cool Whip. Serves 8.

Fastest-Selling Album by a Female

Susan Boyle's (UK) debut album *I Dreamed a Dream* released in November 2009 sold more than a million copies in just 21 days. Her clip of singing the title song on UK TV's *Britain's Got Talent* was the most watched YouTube clip in 2009.

Fastest Growing Plant

Certain species of bamboo grow at a rate of 35 inches a day. (Wouldn't that be eerie to watch!)

Mini Cream Cheese Pie Shells

1 stick butter, softened
½ (8-ounce) package cream cheese, softened
2 cups all-purpose flour

Cream butter and cream cheese; add flour ½ cup at a time till blended well. Refrigerate 30 minutes. Make balls then press into mini muffin tins. May freeze for later, or fill ½ full with pie filling of choice. Bake 15–20 minutes at 350°. Makes 24.

Glorious Grasshopper Pie

24 marshmallows
½ cup milk
¼ cup crème de menthe
1 (16-ounce) carton Cool Whip
1 (8-inch) chocolate pie crust

Over medium heat, melt marshmallows in milk; cool. Add crème de menthe. Fold in Cool Whip. Pour mixture into pie crust and chill. Serves 6–8.

Minty Oreo Pie

2 cups crumbled chocolate Oreos
⅓ cup butter, melted
½ cup crème de menthe
½ gallon vanilla ice cream, softened
Chocolate syrup (optional)

Combine cookie crumbs and butter; press into bottom and sides of a 9-inch pie pan; freeze. Add crème de menthe to ice cream; stir well. Pour into frozen crust. Drizzle with chocolate syrup, if desired. Serves 4–6.

Banana Pudding Pie

2 bananas
1 (9-inch) graham cracker crust
2 cups milk, divided
1 (8-ounce) package cream cheese, softened
1 (3-ounce) package vanilla instant pudding

Slice bananas onto pie crust. In a bowl, mix ½ cup milk with softened cream cheese, mixing until well blended. Add pudding mix and remaining milk; beat slowly about 1 minute. Pour into crust; chill. Serves 6–8.

Berry Whip Pie

1 (14-ounce) can sweetened condensed milk
½ cup lemon juice
1 (8-ounce) container frozen whipped topping
1½ cups assorted fresh berries (blueberries, raspberries, or blackberries)
1 graham cracker pie crust

Combine sweetened condensed milk and lemon juice; mix well. Fold in whipped topping, then berries. Freeze. Take out ½ hour before serving. Or refrigerate about 4 hours till setting up nicely. Serves 8.

Frozen Blueberry Yogurt Pie

2 (8-ounce) cartons blueberry yogurt
1 (8-ounce) carton whipped topping
1 (9-inch) graham cracker crust
1 cup fresh blueberries

Lightly combine yogurt and whipped topping. Pour into pie crust and freeze at least 4 hours. Remove from freezer to refrigerator 20–25 minutes before serving. Top with fresh blueberries. Makes 6–8 servings.

Caribbean Peach Crisp

1 (29-ounce) can sliced peaches with syrup
1 (18¼-ounce) box butter pecan cake mix
½ cup butter, melted
1 cup flaked coconut
1 cup chopped pecans

Layer ingredients in order in ungreased 9x13-inch baking pan. Bake at 325° for about 45 minutes. Serves 10–12.

Quick-As-A-Wink Apple Crisp

1 cup sugar
1 cup all-purpose flour
1 stick butter, melted
1 (21-ounce) can apple pie filling
Cinnamon

Combine sugar, flour, and melted butter. Pour apple pie filling in greased 9x13-inch baking dish. Cover with flour mixture, and sprinkle with cinnamon. Bake at 375° for 35 minutes. Serves 8–10.

Cheesy Apple Cobbler

An interesting touch to an old favorite.

2 (21-ounce) cans apple pie filling
1 (1-pound) package Colby-Jack cheese slices
1 cup self-rising flour
1 cup sugar
2 sticks butter

Spray a 9x13-inch baking dish with cooking spray. Spread pie filling in baking dish; cover with slices of cheese. Mix flour and sugar together; sprinkle over cheese. Cut butter into pats; scatter over entire surface of cobbler mixture. Bake uncovered in 350° oven 45 minutes. Good served with a scoop of vanilla ice cream. Serves 8–10.

No-Fuss Fruit Cobbler

Use any fruit pie filling. Even more amazing served with vanilla ice cream.

1 stick margarine, softened
1 cup sugar
1 cup self-rising flour
1 cup milk
1 (21-ounce) can fruit pie filling

Preheat oven to 350°. Mix all ingredients well. Place in lightly buttered casserole dish. Bake 1 hour. Serves 4–6.

Easy Blackberry Cobbler

2 cups blackberries
1 cup sugar, divided
1 stick butter, softened
1¼ cups Bisquick
1¼ cups milk

Stir blackberries with ¼ cup sugar; set side. In separate bowl, mix remaining ingredients together; pour into a greased casserole dish. Spoon berries on top; do not stir. Bake at 350° for 45 minutes. Serves 8–10.

Editor's Extra: May sub blueberries for blackberries, but use only 1¼ cups.

Fastest Robot to Solve a Rubik's Cube

Rubot II, developed by Peter Redmond (Ireland) solved a scrambled Rubik's Cube within 64 seconds, including the time to scan the initial position, on January 8, 2009, at the Young Scientist show in the Royal Dublin Society.

Crockpot Cherry Cobbler

½ stick butter
½ cup brown sugar
1 teaspoon cinnamon
1 (5-count) can biscuits, baked, torn
2 (21-ounce) cans cherry pie filling

Mix butter, sugar, and cinnamon. Put ½ of biscuits in crockpot. Pour ½ of pie filling over; sprinkle with ½ of sugar mixture. Repeat. Cook on HIGH 2 hours or LOW 4–5 hours. Serve with whipped or ice cream. Serves 10–12.

Oranges in Compote

Simply elegant.

4 large navel oranges, peeled
¼ cup sugar
1 teaspoon cinnamon
Fresh mint for garnish (optional)

Thinly slice oranges. Place in a pretty compote or bowl. Sprinkle with combined sugar and cinnamon. Mix well, cover, and chill until ready to serve. Garnish with a few sprigs of fresh mint, if desired. Serves 4.

Baked Blueberry Dessert

3 tablespoons cornstarch
1½ cups sugar
6 cups fresh blueberries
1 teaspoon grated lemon peel
1 pie pastry

Combine cornstarch and sugar; toss with blueberries and lemon peel. Pour mixture into 1½-quart casserole dish. Roll pastry a little larger than casserole. Cover filling with pastry, fluting edges and cutting slits in top. Bake at 425° for 30–35 minutes, or until bubbly and brown. Makes 8–10 servings.

Lazy Girl's Blueberry Dessert

This is always a hit.

2 (21-ounce) cans blueberry pie filling (or fruit
of choice)
1 (18¼-ounce) package butter cake mix
1 cup chopped pecans
1 stick butter, melted
Whipped topping (optional)

Pour pie filling into ungreased 9x13-inch baking dish. Sprinkle with cake mix, then nuts. Drizzle with butter. Bake at 375° for 35–40 minutes. Serve with whipped topping, if desired. Serves 10–12.

Simple Apple Strudel

Impress your guests with this simple, but tasty treat.

1 sheet frozen puff pastry, thawed
1 (21-ounce) can apple pie filling
1 egg mixed with 1 tablespoon water

Roll pastry into a 12x16-inch rectangle. Spoon filling onto half of short side of pastry to within 1 inch of edge. Roll like a jellyroll. Place seam side down on lightly buttered baking sheet. Tuck ends under to seal. Brush with egg wash. Cut several 2-inch-long slits in top. Bake at 350° for 35 minutes or till golden. Cool 30 minutes. Serve warm. Serves 6.

Peanutty Apple Pizza

1 roll refrigerated sugar cookie dough, room temperature
1 cup peanut butter
2 small Granny Smith apples, peeled, thinly sliced
1 (12-ounce) bottle caramel topping
⅓ cup peanuts, chopped

Spread cookie dough onto a pizza pan. Bake at 350° for 15 minutes till lightly browned; cool. Spread peanut butter over, then layer with apple slices and caramel topping. Sprinkle peanuts on top. Let cool before cutting into wedges. Serves 6–8.

Editor's Extra: Dip apple slices in lemon or pineapple juice to keep from browning.

Quick Apple Roll-Ups

1 (8- to 10-count) package medium flour tortillas
1 (21-ounce) can apple pie filling
¼ cup brown sugar mixed with cinnamon and nutmeg

Lay tortillas on cookie sheet; place 3–4 tablespoons pie filling down center of each tortilla; roll up. Continue till all pie filling is used. Sprinkle tortillas with sugar mixture; cover pan tightly with foil and bake in 350° oven about 15 minutes, just until warm. Serve immediately. Serves 4–6.

Editor's Extra: Great with a scoop of vanilla ice cream on the side.

Crumb-Crusted Baked Apples

These have a special ingredient that makes them tangy and delicious.

5 cups peeled, sliced, apples
½ (3-ounce) package raspberry Jell-O
½ cup butter
¾ cup all-purpose flour
1 cup brown sugar

Place apples in greased baking dish. Sprinkle dry Jell-O over apples. Mix butter, flour, and sugar in food processor till crumbly; sprinkle over apples. Bake in 350° oven 45 minutes. Serves 6.

Fastest Pit Stop

At the 1976 Indianapolis 500, a world record was set for time taken in a pit-stop when Bobby Unser pitted in for four seconds.

Fab more taste

Christmas Cherry Trifle

1 package lady fingers, split
Jelly of choice
1 (6-ounce) package vanilla cook & serve
  pudding mix
1 (16-ounce) can pitted dark sweet cherries,
  drained
Whipped cream

Spread tops and bottoms of lady fingers with jelly; sandwich back together. Place in bottom and around sides of trifle bowl.

Cook pudding as directed. Pour half of pudding over lady fingers. Add a layer of cherries. Repeat layers. Top with whipped cream. Refrigerate till serving time. Serves 6–8.

Lite and Easy Strawberry Trifle

½ bought angel food cake
1 (3-ounce) package sugar-free strawberry
  Jell-O
1 cup water
1 (10-ounce) carton frozen strawberries,
  thawed
1 (8-ounce) carton lite strawberry yogurt

Tear cake into ¾-inch pieces in glass dish. Mix Jell-O with water; refrigerate till slightly thickened. Stir in strawberries and yogurt. Pour over angel food cake pieces; refrigerate. Serves 6–8.

A Very Fine Strawberry Trifle

What's more delightful to serve than this beautiful and delicious trifle? —Nancy Seale

1 (18¼-ounce) box butter cake mix, baked according to package directions
2 (3-ounce) packages vanilla instant pudding, prepared
2 (16-ounce) packages frozen sliced strawberries, thawed
1 (16-ounce) container Cool Whip, thawed

Tear cake into pieces. In a trifle bowl, layer cake pieces, pudding, strawberries, and Cool Whip. Continue twice, ending with Cool Whip.

Strawberries and Cream

Simple and elegant.

2 pints strawberries, halved
½ cup sugar, divided
⅓ cup Grand Marnier
1 teaspoon orange zest
¾ cup heavy cream

Place strawberries in bowl; add ⅓ cup sugar, Grand Marnier, and orange zest. Cover and refrigerate till ready to serve. Whip cream with remaining sugar. Serve in stemmed bowls with whipped cream over berries. Serves 8.

Spanish Cream Dream

Pretty to serve in clear glass dishes to show off the clear bottom and frothy top.

1 envelope unflavored gelatin
6 tablespoons sugar, divided
2 eggs, separated
2 cups milk, divided
1 teaspoon vanilla

Mix gelatin with 4 tablespoons sugar in saucepan. Mix egg yolks with 1 cup milk; add to gelatin mixture; beat well. Cook over low heat, stirring, until gelatin is dissolved. Pour into bowl and add vanilla and remaining cup of milk.

Beat egg whites until frothy, then add remaining 2 tablespoons sugar, a little at a time, beating till soft peaks form. Spoon gelatin mixture into 4–6 individual glass dessert dishes and top with meringue; refrigerate.

Editor's Extra: Pretty to serve with small wafer cookie inserted in top.

Elegant Eggnog with a Spoon

2 envelopes unflavored gelatin
¼ cup sugar
1 quart eggnog, divided
4 teaspoons rum flavoring
1 (8-ounce) carton whipped topping

Combine gelatin and sugar in double boiler. Add 1 cup cold eggnog to mixture and stir over boiling water till sugar is dissolved. Remove from heat and add remaining eggnog and rum flavoring. Chill till slightly thickened. Whip gelatin mixture till light and fluffy; fold in whipped topping. Spoon into individual dessert dishes; chill till firm. Sprinkle with nutmeg, if desired. Makes about 10 dessert cups.

Scrumptious Chocolate Mousse

4 large egg yolks
½ cup sugar
2½ cups whipping cream, divided
6 ounces unsweetened chocolate baking bars,
  chopped

Beat yolks with mixer on high speed till thick, gradually adding sugar. In saucepan over medium heat, heat 1 cup cream till just hot, not boiling. Gradually stir ½ the hot cream into egg mixture, then combine back into hot cream. Cook over low heat about 5 minutes, stirring constantly, until blended and thickened. Let cool 5–10 minutes, then add chocolate chunks, and stir until thickened. Cover and refrigerate for 2 hours, stirring occasionally until chilled.

With mixer on high, beat remaining 1½ cups whipping cream in chilled bowl till stiff. Fold ½ the whipped cream gradually into mixture. Spoon into small dessert bowls. Top with remaining whipped cream. Refrigerate until ready to serve. Serves 6–8.

Oh My Gosh Chocolate Dessert

8 (1-ounce) squares German's chocolate
⅓ cup corn syrup
2 cups whipping cream, divided
1½ cups crushed Oreos
1 cup chopped pecans

Melt chocolate in corn syrup, stirring occasionally. Remove from heat and stir in ½ cup cream; blend well. Refrigerate 30 minutes. Stir in cookies and pecans.

Beat remaining 1½ cups cream till soft peaks form. Gently fold in chocolate mixture to combine. Pour mixture into 12 individual dessert dishes or 1 (9x9-inch) pan; freeze; cut into squares to serve. Top with whipped cream and/or shaved chocolate, if desired.

Fastest Electric Aircraft

Maurizio Cheli (Italy) flew SkySpark light aircraft at the World Air Games 2009 in Turin, Italy. During the eight-minute flight, Cheli achieved a record-breaking maximum speed of 155 mph.

Fab more taste

Fastest Passenger Aircraft on Commercial Flights

The Concorde, a turbojet-powered supersonic transport (SST), entered service in 1976 and continued commercial flights for 27 years.

While commercial jets take eight hours to fly from New York to Paris, the average supersonic flight time on the transatlantic routes was just under 3.5 hours. Concorde had a maximum cruise altitude of 60,039 feet and an average cruise speed of Mach 2.02, about 1,155 knots (1,334 mph), more than twice the speed of conventional aircraft.

Ice Cream Oreo Squares

1 stick butter, melted
1 (19-ounce) package Oreos, crushed, reserve ½ cup
½ gallon vanilla ice cream, softened
2 (8-ounce) jars fudge sauce
1 (16-ounce) carton Cool Whip

Combine butter and Oreos and press into a 9x13-inch pan. Spread ice cream over crust; add a layer of fudge sauce, completely covering ice cream. Top with Cool Whip. Sprinkle with remaining ½ cup Oreo crumbs and any remaining fudge sauce. Freeze till ready to serve. Makes about 24 squares.

Old-Fashioned Rice Pudding

1 cup cooked rice
3 tablespoons butter, melted
1 cup milk
2 eggs, well beaten
⅓ cup sugar

Combine all ingredients; mix well. Spread in greased baking dish. Bake at 350° till golden brown, 35–40 minutes. Serve warm.

Heavenly Rice Dessert

2 cups cooked rice
½ cup sugar
1 (8-ounce) can pineapple tidbits, drained
1 cup whipping cream, whipped

Combine rice, sugar, and pineapple; refrigerate 1 hour or more. Just before serving, fold in whipped cream. Serves 6.

Perfect Homemade Cream Puffs

These are delicious when filled with vanilla, chocolate, or lemon pudding, or Cool Whip.

1 cup water
1 stick butter
¼ teaspoon salt
1 cup all-purpose flour
4 eggs

Boil water, butter, and salt in a heavy pan over medium heat; add flour all at once. Stir constantly over low heat till dough forms a smooth ball (just a minute or so). Remove from heat; add eggs, one at a time, beating well after each. Drop by spoonfuls onto ungreased baking pan. Smooth into balls or oblong shapes. Bake at 425° for 20–25 minutes; place on wire rack to cool. Cut tops off and fill with whipped cream, pudding, or filling (like chicken salad) of choice. Refrigerate. Makes about 12.

Strawberry Fluff

A delightful summer dessert.

1 (10-ounce) package sweetened frozen
  strawberries, sliced
2 large egg whites, unbeaten
½ cup sugar
1 tablespoon fresh lemon juice
1 cup very cold whipping cream

Beat partially thawed strawberries, egg whites, sugar, and lemon juice in a large mixing bowl on high speed about 5 minutes, till thick. Whip cream and fold into strawberry mixture. Freeze in casserole dish. Serves 6.

Editor's Extra: This works well in a baked pie shell for a nice frozen strawberry pie.

Easy Apricot Fluff

2 tablespoons sugar
1 cup whipping cream, whipped
1 (8-ounce) jar apricot baby food with tapioca

Add sugar to whipped cream; fold in baby food. Spoon into stemmed glasses. Refrigerate till time to serve. Serves 4–5.

Luscious Lemon Curd

So good on fruit, bagels, in a pie shell with whipped topping . . . nice to take as a gift in a jar!

¼ cup freshly squeezed lemon juice
6 tablespoons butter
1 cup sugar
3 eggs

Put all but eggs in double boiler or metal bowl over pot of simmering water; stir until butter melts and sugar dissolves. In separate bowl, beat eggs thoroughly. Add a little lemon mixture to eggs, stirring constantly. Pour into remaining lemon mixture, stirring constantly, and continue to cook till curd is thick. Remove from heat and refrigerate when cool. Makes 2 cups.

Lemon Cooler

Easy and refreshing.

½ cup fresh lemon juice, strained
2 cups sugar
4 cups milk or half and half
Lemon slices (optional)

Mix ingredients well. Pour into stainless steel bowl and freeze for 4 hours or more. Spoon into serving bowls and garnish with a slice of lemon, if desired. Serves 6–8.

Editor's Extra: Add a teaspoon or so of lemon zest for more robust lemony flavor.

Pineapple Buttermilk Sherbet

1 cup buttermilk
1 (8-ounce) can crushed pineapple, undrained
1 cup sugar
1 teaspoon vanilla
2 cups heavy cream, whipped

Mix first 4 ingredients. Freeze till slushy. Fold whipped cream into mixture. Freeze, stirring once or twice while freezing. Serves 6 or more.

Wafflewich

4 waffles, toasted
½ cup vanilla or strawberry ice cream, softened
Strawberry glaze

Spread 2 waffles with ice cream. Top with remaining 2 toasted waffles; freeze. To serve, slightly thaw and cut each wafflewich diagonally into 4 wedges, and drizzle with strawberry glaze. Serves 4.

Fastest Internet Speed

Internet speed is measured in bits per second (k), so the larger the number, the **faster** the service.

- Dial-up connection can only reach speeds up to 56k.
- Cable connection will give you a speed of about 400k.
- DSL (short for Digital Subscriber Link), service is usually 450 to 650k.
- Average speed for satellite connection is 600k or higher.
- Fiber-optic connection is so **fast** that its speed is measured in megabits rather than bits. With speeds of up to 30 megabits (that's 30 million bits), fiber-optic service is definitely the **fastest** way to connect to the Internet today. Unfortunately, due to limited availability, it's not an option for many users.

Fastest Roller Coasters

1. Formula Rossa, 194 mph, Farrari World on Yas Island in Abu Dhabi

2. Ring Racer F1, 135 mph, Norburgring, Nurburg, Germany (soon to open)

3. Kingda Ka, 128 mph, Six Flags Great Adventure, Jackson, NJ

4. Top Thrill Dragster, 120 mph, Cedar Point, Sandusky, OH

5. Dodonpa, 107 mph, Fuji, Yamanashi, Japan

Cherries Flambé

1 (16-ounce) can dark sweet cherries, drained, reserve juice
2 teaspoons cornstarch
¼ cup Kirsch
½ cup cherry-flavored brandy
1 quart vanilla ice cream

Bring cherry juice to a boil. Mix cornstarch and Kirsch till smooth, and add to juice. Cook slowly till thickened and clear. Add cherries and cook 2 more minutes. Pour brandy over and ignite. Carefully serve (while flaming) over vanilla ice cream. Serves 6–8.

Peach and Brickle Sundae

1 (16-ounce) package frozen peach slices, partially thawed
¼ cup dark rum
½ teaspoon almond extract
1 quart vanilla ice cream
1 cup crushed brickle bits

Reserve some peach slices for garnish. Process remaining peaches, rum, and extract till almost smooth. Scoop ice cream into serving dish; pour peach sauce over ice cream. Top with crushed brickle bits and peach slices. Serves 6–8.

Make-Your-Own Oreo Ice Cream

½ gallon vanilla ice cream, softened
1 (16-ounce) package Oreos, crumbled
1 (12-ounce) carton Cool Whip
½ cup chopped pecans (optional)

Combine all ingredients; pack into any size freezer containers; freeze. Ready to serve.

Kahlúa Ice Cream Quickie

1 tablespoon brown sugar
⅓ cup Kahlúa
1 quart vanilla ice cream, softened

Mix sugar and Kahlúa together till sugar dissolves; combine all in blender. Freeze in container or in individual dishes. Garnish servings with a dollop of whipped cream, cherry, and toasted chopped nuts, if desired. Serves 4–6.

Creamy Kahlúa Sauce

1½ pints heavy cream
¼ cup Kahlúa
4 drops red food coloring
1 (7-ounce) jar marshmallow crème
Strawberries, stemmed, cut in half

Mix cream with Kahlúa and food coloring. Beat till stiff. Blend in marshmallow crème. Layer strawberries in wine glasses with sauce. Should be made the same day you serve it. Makes 4 cups.

Editor's Extra: Good to dip whole strawberries in as an appetizer.

The Easiest and Best Vanilla Ice Cream

1 pint half-and-half
1 pint whipping cream
1 (14-ounce) can sweetened condensed milk
2 tablespoons vanilla

Combine all ingredients; mix well. Pour into ice cream freezer container; freeze according to manufacturer's instructions. Serves 8 or more.

Strawberry Fantasy Ice Cream Sauce

½ stick butter
½ cup sugar
Zest of 1 lemon
½ cup Kirsch
1 pint strawberries, sliced

Melt butter with sugar in skillet, stirring till sugar is dissolved and bubbly. Stir in zest and Kirsch. Cook, stirring till bubbly again; add strawberries. Remove from heat and serve warm over ice cream. Serves 6 or more.

Editor's Extra: Kirsch is cherry-flavored brandy. You could sub brandy or cherry juice, or both.

Camp-Out Banana Canoes

Fun to make and yummy to eat!

4 bananas
4 teaspoons mini chocolate chips
40 mini marshmallows

Cut bananas on inside curve through skin and halfway into banana. Carefully open enough to form a pocket. Spoon a teaspoon of chocolate chips and 10 mini marshmallows into each canoe. Now make 4 canoe forms out of heavy-duty foil to place banana canoes in for grilling. Place on grill, covered, over medium heat. After 6–10 minutes, the chocolate should be oozy and the marshmallows should be browned on top. Yum!

More **Fast** and **Fabulous**

FIVE ★ STAR

Extra Help

Cooking Techniques

Bake: To cook by dry heat in an oven.

Blanching: Vegetables or fruit are immersed briefly into boiling water and plunged into iced water to halt the cooking process. Blanching preserves texture, color, and flavor, or is used to loosen skin.

Baste: To moisten, usually meats, with melted butter, sauce, or pan drippings while cooking.

Braise: To cook, especially meats, covered, in a small amount of liquid.

Broil: To cook by direct exposure to intense heat such as a flame or an electric heating unit.

Clarify: To remove impurities from melted butter or margarine by allowing sediment to settle, then pouring off clear yellow liquid.

Cream: To blend shortening, butter, margarine, usually softened, or sometimes oil, with granulated or crushed ingredients until mixture is soft and creamy.

Deglaze: To heat stock, wine, or other liquid in pan in which meat has been cooked, mixing with pan juices and sediment to form a gravy or sauce base.

Dredge: To coat completely with flour, bread crumbs, etc.

Fold in: To blend a delicate frothy mixture into a heavier one so that none of the lightness or volume is lost. Using a rubber spatula, turn under and bring up and over, rotating bowl ¼ turn after each folding motion.

Garnish: To decorate or enhance food before serving.

Julienne: To cut vegetables, fruit, etc., into long thin strips.

Marinate: To soak, usually in a highly seasoned oil-acid solution to flavor and/or tenderize food.

Pan-broil or **Pan-fry:** To cook in a skillet or pan using a very small amount of fat to prevent sticking.

Parboil: To partially cook in boiling water. Most parboiled foods require additional cooking with or without other ingredients.

Plump: To soak fruits, usually dried, in liquid until puffy and softened.

Purée: To reduce the pulp of cooked fruits and vegetables to a smooth and thick liquid by straining or blending.

Reduce: To boil stock, gravy, or other liquid until the volume is reduced, the liquid is thickened, and the flavor is intensified.

Render: To cook meat or meat trimmings at low temperature until fat melts and can be drained and strained.

(continued)

(Cooking Techniques continued)

Roast: To cook by dry heat in an oven or over hot coals.

Sauté: To cook in a skillet containing a small amount of hot cooking oil. Sautéed foods should be stirred frequently.

Score: To make shallow cuts diagonally in parallel lines, especially in meat.

Simmer: To cook in or with a liquid at or just below the boiling point.

Stew: To simmer, usually meats and vegetables, for a long period of time. Also used to tenderize meats.

Stir-fry: To cook small pieces of vegetables and/or meat in a small amount of oil in a wok or skillet over high heat, stirring constantly, until tender-crisp.

A Little About Seasonings

Seasonings are used to flavor food. ***Salt***, *the most common seasoning, is a mineral. (It is not an herb or a spice.) Salt enhances flavor using the food's own natural flavor. Spices and herbs add to the flavor of food.* ***Spices*** *are made from the bark, root, stem, seed, or fruit of a plant.* ***Herbs*** *are the leaves of a plant and can be used fresh or dried.*

COMMON SPICES:

Allspice: A pungent aromatic spice, that is whole or powdered. It is excellent in marinades and good in curries.

Caraway seed: Use whole seeds in breads, especially rye, and with cheese, sauerkraut, and cabbage dishes.

Cardamom: A member of the ginger family, with a strong, unique taste. It is a common ingredient in Indian cooking.

Celery seed: Use whole or ground in salad dressing, sauces, pickles, meat, eggs, cheese, and fish dishes.

Chili powder: Made from dried red chili peppers, this spice ranges from mild to fiery depending on the type of chili pepper used. Good in Mexican cooking.

Cinnamon: Ground from the bark of the cinnamon tree; delicious in desserts as well as savory dishes.

Curry powder: A blend of several spices, this gives Indian cooking its characteristic flavor.

Cumin: A staple spice in Mexican cooking. Cumin is the second most popular spice in the world after black pepper.

Garlic: The bulb of the plant is used (raw or cooked) and has a characteristic pungent, spicy flavor that mellows and sweetens considerably with cooking.

(continued)

(A Little About Seasonings continued)

Ginger: A sweet, pungent addition to desserts or oriental-style dishes. Grate the fresh root, or use dried ground.

Mustard: Ground mustard seed brings a sharp bite to sauces or may be sprinkled sparingly over poultry or other foods.

Nutmeg: Use whole spice or a bit of freshly ground for flavor in beverages, breads, and desserts.

Paprika: Made from the dried fruits of bell peppers or chili peppers. The highest quality and most expensive paprika comes from Spain. Hungary is a source of cheaper paprika.

Pepper: Black and white pepper from the pepperberry or peppercorn, whether whole, ground, or cracked, is the most commonly used spice in or on any food.

Poppy seed: Use these tiny, nutty-flavored seeds in salad dressings, breads, cakes, or as a flavorful garnish.

COMMON HERBS:

Add dried herbs at the beginning and during cooking. Add fresh herbs only at the end of cooking or upon serving.

Bay Leaf: This aromatic leaf is often used in soups, stews, braises, and pâtés. The fresh leaves are very mild and do not develop their full flavor until after picking and drying.

Basil: Many species of basil exist, but the most popular is sweet basil. The strong, clove-like flavor is essential to many Italian recipes, and it is paired most often with tomatoes.

Oregano: Oregano has a warm, aromatic scent and robust taste. It is commonly used in Italian and Greek cuisine.

Parsley: There are two types of parsley. Flat leaf or Italian is used primarily in cooking because of its more robust flavor, and curly parsley is used primarily for garnish.

Sage: Its subtle lemon, yet minty aroma and taste is most closely associated with French cuisine.

Rosemary: Has a tea-like aroma and a piney flavor. Crush leaves by hand or with a mortar and pestle before using.

Thyme: Often used to flavor meats, soups, and stews. While flavorful, it does not overpower and blends well with other herbs and spices.

What does it mean?

Low Fat: A food with 3 grams of fat or less per serving.

Light or Lite: Food has ⅓ fewer calories than a comparable product.

Low Calorie: A food with fewer than 40 calories per serving.

Low Sodium: The food contains 140 mg or less per serving.

More **Fast** and **Fabulous** FIVE★STAR Index